The Music
Library

The History of
Rock and Roll

Other books in this series include:

The Music
Library

The History of
Rock and Roll

by Stuart A. Kallen

LUCENT
BOOKS®

THOMSON

GALE

San Diego • Detroit • New York • San Francisco • Cleveland • New Haven, Conn. • Waterville, Maine • London • Munich

On Cover: Pink Floyd in concert.

© 2003 by Lucent Books. Lucent Books is an imprint of The Gale Group, Inc., a division of Thomson Learning, Inc.

Lucent Books® and Thomson Learning™ are trademarks used herein under license.

For more information, contact
Lucent Books
27500 Drake Rd.
Farmington Hills, MI 48331-3535
Or you can visit our Internet site at http://www.gale.com

LIBRARY OF CONGRESS CATALOGING-IN-PUBLICATION DATA

Kallen, Stuart A., 1955–
    The history of rock and roll / by Stuart A. Kallen.
        p. cm. — (The music library)
Includes bibliographical references (p.) and index.
Contents: The roots of rock — The Beatles and the British invasion — Sweet sixties soul — Folk music turns psychedelic — Rock and roll superstars — The rise of punk rock — Rock's next generation.
    ISBN 1-59018-126-3 (alk. paper)
    1. Rock music—History and criticism—Juvenile literature. [1. Rock music—History and criticism.] I. Title. II. Music library (San Diego, Calif.)
    ML3534 .K33 2003
    781.66'09—dc21

        2002003923

Printed in the United States of America

• Contents •

• Foreword •

In the nineteenth century English novelist Charles Kingsley wrote, "Music speaks straight to our hearts and spirits, to the very core and root of our souls. . . . Music soothes us, stirs us up . . . melts us to tears." As Kingsley stated, music is much more than just a pleasant arrangement of sounds. It is the resonance of emotion, a joyful noise, a human endeavor that can soothe the spirit or excite the soul. Musicians can also imitate the expressive palate of the earth, from the violent fury of a hurricane to the gentle flow of a babbling brook.

The word music is derived from the fabled Greek muses, the children of Apollo who ruled the realms of inspiration and imagination. Composers have long called upon the muses for help and insight. Music is not merely the result of emotions and pleasurable sensations, however.

Music is a discipline subject to formal study and analysis. It involves the juxtaposition of creative elements such as rhythm, melody, and harmony with intellectual aspects of composition, theory, and instrumentation. Like painters

mixing red, blue, and yellow into thousands of colors, musicians blend these various elements to create classical symphonies, jazz improvisations, country ballads, and rock-and-roll tunes.

Throughout centuries of musical history, individual musical elements have been blended and modified in infinite ways. The resulting sounds may convey a whole range of moods, emotions, reactions, and messages. Music, then, is both an expression and reflection of human experience and emotion.

The foundations of modern musical styles were laid down by the first ancient musicians who used wood, rocks, animal skins—and their own bodies—to re-create the sounds of the natural world in which they lived. With their hands, their feet, and their very breath they ignited the passions of listeners and moved them to their feet. The dancing, in turn, had a mesmerizing and hypnotic effect that allowed people to transcend their worldly concerns. Through music they could achieve a level of shared experience that could not be found in other forms of communication. For this reason, music has always been part of religious endeavors, from ancient Egyptian religious ceremonies to modern Christian masses. And it has inspired dance movements from kings and queens spinning the minuet to punk rockers slamming together in a mosh pit.

By examining musical genres ranging from Western classical music to rock and roll, readers will find a new understanding of old music and develop an appreciation for new sounds. Books in Lucent's Music Library focus on the music, the musicians, the instruments, and on music's place in cultural history. The songs and artists examined may be easily found in the CD and sheet music collections of local libraries so that readers may study and enjoy the music covered in the books. Informative sidebars, annotated bibliographies, and complete indexes highlight the text in each volume and provide young readers with many opportunities for further discussion and research.

There's Good Rockin' Tonight

Rock and roll: Those three words are understood by people in almost every nation on Earth. They describe a type of music—and an attitude—that made history. What started out as a new style of dance music for teenage baby boomers during 1950s America transformed the cultural—and even political—landscape of much of the world by the end of the 1960s. Never before in history has a style of music come along that so quickly and so completely changed the world.

Rock-and-roll music has come to define what it means to be a teenager in the modern world. It affects the way people look, dress, act, and talk. From the very beginning, rock and roll and the musicians who performed it challenged existing social norms, provoking defiance, disrespect for authority, and, at times, revolution among its fans.

Even from its earliest days, the language of rock separated its listeners from the rest of the world—especially teenagers from their parents. While creating this divide, what became known as "the generation gap" during the sixties, it also created a community of like-minded enthusiasts who could instantly bond with one another. As anyone who has ever attended a rock concert knows, it becomes easy to talk to a perfect stranger simply because he or she shares a common interest in the band that is onstage.

Based on the Blues

Although rock and roll has had complex implications for the entire world, it is some of the simplest music around. Often described as consisting of three chords and an attitude, most rock songs are based on simple note patterns that originated in blues music developed during the nineteenth century. But those ingeniously played three chords can be used behind an infinite number of melodies that can be woven into the fabric of the song with lead guitars, bass guitars, horns, keyboards, and other instruments. Throw in a few extra chords here and there, and add poetry in the form of rock lyrics sung as a vocal melody, and one has the basis for about 95 percent of all rock songs.

To write rock and roll off as simplistic, however, would be ill advised. Like the United States, the land of its birth, rock and roll is a melting pot, a synthesis of sounds that include jazz, country, blues, ragtime, gospel, swing, classical, and ethnic music from Africa, Europe, and elsewhere. And as more than a sum of its parts, rock music can encompass many different sounds, including the angry one-chord buzz-saw sound of a punk band, the experimental "sound pictures" of Pink Floyd, the sweet harmonies of NSync, or the sampled sounds and rhythmic hip hop of rap.

Rock music can embrace so many sounds because it is a child of technology; indeed, its very sound through the decades has been determined by advances in musical and recording equipment. Although electric guitars and amplifiers were invented during the 1930s, they did not become widely available until the 1950s. The first Fender Stratocaster—a favorite of rock guitar players even today—was not commercially produced until 1954—around the same time that rock music first burst onto the scene. By 1959 Americans were snapping up almost half a million guitars a year, and by 1963 Fender alone was selling fifteen hundred guitars a week. Amateur musicians who, in another era, might have learned to play the violin or trumpet, were now latching onto electric guitars.

And as technology drove the music, the music drove technology. During the 1960s

British rock musician Eric Clapton holds a 1956 Fender Stratocaster guitar, the instrument favored by rock-and-roll performers beginning in the mid-1950s.

the Beatles worked in the studio for months to produce unusual sound effects, sometimes by physically manipulating recording tape. By the 1970s similar sounds could be obtained by the push of a button or by stepping on an effects pedal. These inventions transformed rock music again with the sounds of the distorted "fuzz" tone, the wavelike phase shifter, the wa-wa, and other noises.

By the late seventies the availability of electric synthesizers and drum machines ushered in the disco and New Wave era. The eighties introduced the computer to rock and roll, along with an infinite variety of digitally produced sounds, and by the nineties sampling and other computer tricks took rock to another level of complexity.

Music Is Love

As the technology for producing it became cheaper, rock and roll invaded nearly every aspect of life, and today rock music is everywhere. It is played in school classrooms and at world-class sporting events such as the Olympics and the Superbowl. Rock music blasts from radios, stereos, CD players, and even cell phones from Bangkok to Paris to Cleveland. It propels a multibillion-dollar industry dominated by some of the largest corporations in the world.

Rock music acts as a universal language among fans, allowing them to enjoy songs together even if they otherwise speak different tongues. As a source of joy and inspiration, rock and roll has put an indelible stamp upon the world. Although not all of rock's influences have been positive, the music has acted as a point from which people can recognize their universal humanity. Rock singer David Crosby once sang that music is love, and while some may not agree with that statement, there is a lot to love in a style of music that has brought so much happiness to so many people in so many places throughout the years.

Chapter One

The Roots of Rock

R ock and roll's most distinctive element is rhythm, and nearly every musical style that helped spawn rock music has a powerful beat that makes people want to dance. The roots of rock rhythm were born centuries ago in African tribal music, with its strong drumbeats that highlighted the second and fourth beats, or "backbeats," in each four-beat measure. Also known as syncopation, when the backbeat is emphasized, this type of rhythm makes people want to clap their hands, tap their feet, and dance. In a very real sense, this syncopation is the heartbeat of rock and roll.

Another aspect of tribal music that found its way into rock and roll was the traditional vocal style known as call and response, in which a song leader sings a line and a group of singers repeats it. This singing technique was brought to American shores by black slaves who modified it for use in Christian gospel singing. The call and response style was also used in work songs, known as field hollers.

By the end of the nineteenth century, African American musicians were using modified call and response, syncopation, and field hollers in a new style of music called blues. Blues songs took as their subject matter the appalling prejudice, discrimination, and poverty under which most African Americans survived at the time. The lyrics gave musical expression to the broken hearts, loneliness, homelessness, and intolerance that people routinely faced. These songs, which incorporated three basic chords with their flexible gliding melodies, or "blue notes," lie at the roots of rock.

By the end of the nineteenth century, the traditional forms of black music had been adapted by southern white musicians, who added their own musical traditions, such as European marching band music and traditional English country ballads, to the mix. This musical synthesis gave rise to ragtime,

The African Roots of Blues

In Rockin' in Time: A Social History of Rock and Roll, *David P. Szatmary explains how traditional African music gave birth to the blues.*

The blues were an indigenous creation of black slaves who adapted their African musical heritage to the American environment. . . .

Torn . . . from their homes in West Africa . . . and forced into . . . [slavery], Africans retained continuity with their past through music. Their voices glided between the lines of the more rigid European musical scale to create a distinctive new sound. . . .

The music involved calculated repetitions. In this call-and-response, used often to decrease the monotony of work, one slave would call or play a lead part, and his fellow workers would follow with the same phrase or an embellishment of it until another took the lead. As one observer wrote in 1845, "Our black oarsmen made the woods echo to their song. One of them, taking the lead, first improvised a verse, paying compliments to his master's family, and to a celebrated black beauty of the neighborhood, who was compared to the 'red bird.' The other five then joined in the chorus, always repeating the same words." Some slaves, especially those from the Bantu tribe, whooped, or jumped octaves, during the call-and-response which served as a basis for field hollers.

Probably most important, the slaves, accustomed to dancing and singing to the beat of drums in Africa, emphasized rhythm over harmony. In a single song they clapped, danced, and slapped their bodies in several different rhythms, compensating for the absence of drums, which were outlawed by plantation owners, who feared that the instrument would be used to coordinate slave insurrections. One ex-slave, writing in 1853, called the polyrhythmic practice "patting juba." It was performed by "striking the right shoulder with one hand, the left with the other—all the while keeping time with the feet and singing."

which combined European-style melodies with African American syncopation, and country, or "hillbilly," music, which was essentially the blues as interpreted by white people in the rural South.

All That Jazz

Jazz, a combination of blues, ragtime, Mardi Gras marches, and European military music, was another musical stream that fed into the flow of rock and roll. Predating early rock by several decades, jazz music is based on improvisation—that is, the musicians made up melodies on the spot rather than reading notes from previously written music scores. Improvised musical passages are known as riffs or licks in jazz, and those terms are also used to describe hot rock and roll.

Improvising is also known as jamming. When jazz musicians jam, they compose and play at the same time. This allows individual players in a group to show off their musical skills and creativity. Jazz players believe there are an infinite number of melodies that can be played within any song. Improvisers often imitate singing with their instruments, gliding, swooping, and soaring through seemingly endless cascades of notes. Musicians may "bend" notes (waver between two different tones) to obtain a "blues" quality.

Stars such as Louis Armstrong and Benny Goodman were regaled much as rock musicians are today. Jazz musicians sold millions of records, toured

concert halls across the country, and had a strong effect on American culture, influencing the way people dressed, danced, and even talked.

Boogie-Woogie Beat

By the 1940s jazz was mostly played by big bands with more than a dozen players. Smaller combos featuring a guitar, stand-up bass, piano, drums, and a horn section were able to take the jazz style and blend it with blues into another new form of music known as rhythm and blues (R&B). This style featured a strong backbeat, hot improvised solos by individual

Louis Jordan originated up-tempo, hard-driving, blues-based dance music called jump blues that was a precursor to rock and roll.

players, and blueslike lyrics shouted over the music.

Rhythm-and-blues pianists were often influenced by a playing style—popular during the 1920s—known as stride, in which players use their left hand to play percussive, "striding" midrange chords and bass notes while their right hand "tickles" out the melody on the upper keys. By the 1940s this style was known as boogie-woogie, and it was often accompanied by a stand-up bass playing the "walking" bass line.

The boogie-woogie style found a new form when utilized by band leader Louis Jordan, who originated the "jump blues"—an up-tempo, hard-driving, blues-based dance music. Jordan immortalized the eminently danceable jump blues style during the mid-1940s with best-selling songs such as "Caldonia" and "Choo Choo Ch'Boogie."

There's Good Rockin' Tonight

Jordan's jump blues inspired other musicians, such as Wynonie Harris, an R&B singer who would one day be credited with pioneering rock and roll. In December 1947 Harris electrified listeners, both black and white, with his recording of "Good Rockin' Tonight." This number features a rollicking boogie-woogie piano; loud hand claps on the backbeat, reminiscent of gospel music; and a walking bass line behind Harris's vociferous vocals. The Hoy Hoy website describes the importance of the song:

This record is what started the whole "rocking" craze in blues in the late 1940's, which would eventually lead to the greatest musical revolution of all time. This is probably the most important record in the history of rock and roll—without this record, rock and roll probably never would have happened.[1]

"Rock Around the Clock"

The point at which rock and roll probably became a musical style all its own came in 1951, when a Philadelphia-based country singer named Bill Haley recorded a rocking R&B song titled "Rocket 88." Although the record failed to sell in large numbers, Haley opened his show with the song when he played in local barrooms. The song went over well with the crowds, so Haley augmented his set with a jump blues song called "Rock the Joint." These songs were so well received that Haley dumped his country band with their cowboy outfits and hired a tight combo of jazz musicians, which he named the Comets. Haley taught the band choreographed steps he had seen performed by black R&B groups, and they rehearsed after listening to records of African American jump blues bands.

Haley hardly looked like someone destined for stardom. Dressed in a plaid jacket with a lock of hair falling over his forehead, the stout Haley looked rather like someone's goofy uncle, but after his recording of "Crazy Man

Crazy" went to number twelve on the *Billboard* pop charts, Bill Haley and his Comets became minor stars along the East Coast.

The growing popularity of the Comets landed Haley a contract with Decca, a major record label, which released the novelty song "(We're Gonna) Rock Around the Clock" in 1954. The song, written by a sixty-three-year-old professional tunesmith named Max Freedman, was a minor hit for Haley, lasting only one week on the *Billboard* charts after peaking at number twenty-three. But then the song appeared over the opening credits of the 1955 movie *Blackboard Jungle,* and it became a best-selling rock-and-roll phenomenon.

Blackboard Jungle was a movie about juvenile delinquents who terrorize teachers—and each other—in an inner-city school. And when 1950s teenagers in the audience heard the title song, they were so amazed by the sound that it provoked near riots in some theaters. There was nothing apparently revolutionary in the song's lyrics; in *Flowers in the Dustbin: The Rise of Rock and Roll, 1947–1977,* James Miller describes why the song made such a huge impact:

> Wishing to use the song as a symbol of youthful mayhem and menace, [the producers of the movie] decided to add a crucial new dimension to the

Bill Haley and his Comets became stars performing "Rock Around the Clock," the first rock-and-roll hit.

music—sheer volume. In those years, it was customary for Hollywood producers to lower the levels of the bass and treble on the music used on soundtracks, lest the audience in theaters be deafened by the giant loudspeakers behind the screen. For *Blackboard Jungle,* however, the producers ran . . . "Rock Around the Clock" wide open, letting the music hit listeners in the gut.

In a large theater, "(We're Gonna) Rock Around the Clock" was loud—for most people, it was the loudest music they had ever heard. The volume of the beat added to the menace of the scene on screen. A crude but effective symbolic association was put into play: the louder the sound, the more strongly it would connote power, aggression, violence. Haley's band may sound quaint when compared to Led Zeppelin or the Sex Pistols: but heavy metal and punk both have their origins in the shock waves produced by the soundtrack of *Blackboard Jungle.*[2]

Although adults were appalled by what they perceived as wild, scary music, teenagers loved it. By the beginning of 1956 "(We're Gonna) Rock Around the Clock" had sold a phenomenal 6 million copies. No record had ever sold this well, and demand continued for decades, with more than 25 million copies of the record being sold. By the end of the twentieth century, "(We're Gonna) Rock Around the Clock" would be the second-best-selling single in history. Only Bing Crosby's "White Christmas" would sell more copies.

Elvis Is All Shook Up

While Haley rode the rock tidal wave, a new breed of white southern bad boys were combining the sounds of rock and "hillbilly" country into a style known as rockabilly. And the center of the rockabilly revolution was Sun Records, a Memphis recording studio owned by Sam Phillips, a music lover who would lend a sympathetic ear to nearly any blues, bluegrass, or R&B musician who came to his studio. Phillips recorded singles for then-unknown musicians such as B.B. King, Little Milton, Howling Wolf, and Ike Turner.

As much as Phillips loved the music of these artists, he faced a problem promoting their records because of racial prejudice: White-owned radio stations refused to play records by these black musicians, and white store owners would not sell them. Phillips, therefore, was continually looking for a white singer who could sing in the manner of black R&B artitsts. As his partner Marion Keisker recalled, "Sam had said, several times, that he wished he could find a white singer with the soul and feeling and the kind of voice to do what was then identified as rhythm & blues songs."[3] Phillips's wish came true when a truck driver named Elvis Presley from

Alan Freed's Moondog Show

The first man to play rock and roll on the radio—and to use the term to describe the music—was Alan Freed.

Freed, a seminal figure in the history of rock, began spinning R&B and early rock records on his *Moondog Show* on WJW radio station in Cleveland, Ohio, in 1951. Freed originally hosted a classical music show, but when a local record store owner told him that hundreds of white teens were buying R&B records by black artists, the disc jockey persuaded WJW to let him spin some of the popular records after midnight.

Freed inaugurated *The Moondog Show* on a fifty-thousand-watt clear channel in Cleveland. The signal was so strong that it skipped across the stratosphere to a vast area of the Midwest. Teenagers could tune in from rural towns, big cities, and suburbs to hear Freed spinning records, chattering wildly, and beating on a Cleveland phone book with a drumstick. Freed's show proved so popular that he was signed by WINS in New York City in 1954, where he hosted Alan Freed's *Rock and Roll Party*.

Freed was also the first person to produce rock-and-roll concerts featuring six or seven acts. Some of these events turned violent, however. At a rock show in Boston, police upset the crowd by turning on the house lights, thereby interrupting the concert. Afterward, members of the audience went on a spree, breaking windows and fighting. One boy was killed, and others were severely beaten. Freed was charged with inciting a riot and anarchy. It took him several years—and a great deal of money—to get the trumped-up charges thrown out of court.

Tupelo, Mississippi, came to the studio to make a demo record.

In the spring of 1954 Presley recorded "That's All Right," backed by seasoned country performers guitarist Scotty Moore and bassist Bill Black. Although Presley lacked experience, the confidence in his voice and his ringing rhythm guitar sounded unlike anything Phillips had ever heard. The single was released in June, backed by a rocked-up version of the bluegrass song "Blue Moon of Kentucky," and it became a minor hit in Memphis. But it was Presley's performance onstage that created a sensation. When crowds of teenage girls saw Elvis play live, they went into hysterics, screaming, yelling, and crying as the singer gyrated his hips, wiggled his legs, and jiggled around the stage.

Elvis's popularity onstage in turn drove the success of his records. When Presley released the emotion-charged "Heartbreak Hotel" on April 21, 1956, it shot to the top of the *Billboard* charts. He followed that song with a string of hits that made him a household name. For fifty-five of the next one hundred weeks, Elvis would have the best-selling records in America with "Hound Dog," "Don't Be Cruel," "All Shook Up," "Love Me Tender," and others. Most of America, however, was still not ready for Elvis. When he appeared on *The Ed Sullivan Show,* the most popular variety show on television, he was shown only from the waist up. His bump-and-grind dancing was deemed too sensual for mass consumption.

Elvis's brand of rockabilly and rock and roll inspired a generation of teenagers. Many of these teens, including future Beatle John Lennon and the

Elvis Presley's brand of rockabilly and rock and roll, along with his wild on-stage gyrations, inspired a generation of teenagers.

youngster who would one day be known as Bob Dylan, found a unique sense of freedom and rebellion in Presley's music. As Dylan later said about the exhilaration he felt the first time he heard Presley's voice booming from the radio, "I just knew that I wasn't going to work for anybody; nobody was going to be my boss. . . . Hearing [Elvis] for the first time was like busting out of jail."[4]

"Whole Lotta Shakin'"

Until Haley and Presley came along, there had been no music specifically aimed at teenagers, who were simply expected to listen to the songs that were popular with their parents. And at the time, pop music in America was dominated by syrupy orchestral arrangements and crooning singers wholesomely dressed in sweaters or formal clothes. For example, the week Elvis's "Heartbreak Hotel" was released it competed on the charts with the corny "Hot Diggity" by Perry Como and a sugary instrumental, "Lisbon Antigua," by the Nelson Riddle Orchestra. Other hits at that time included "Love Is a Many Splendored Thing" and "Yellow Rose of Texas." In such a conservative climate, when the Sun Records alumnus Jerry Lee "Killer" Lewis, released the delirious "Whole Lotta Shakin'" and "Great Balls of Fire" in 1957, he might as well have dropped to Earth from outer space for the effect he had on the teenage audience.

While Elvis's dance moves had shocked parents, nobody was ready for Lewis, who performed in a leopard-skin jacket with his long blond hair flapping in his face. Furthermore, Lewis's onstage antics, such as physical abuse of his grand pianos, was shocking to many. He danced on top, played the upper keys with the heels of his shoes, beat the bass notes with his head, tore off keys and threw them into the audience, and, on occasion, pushed the heavy, expensive instruments off the stage, breaking them into splinters. And there was more, as Lewis states: "One night I just filled a Coca-Cola bottle with gasoline and took it [on stage] with me. . . . When I got through doing 'Great Balls of Fire,' I sprinkled some of the gasoline inside the piano and threw a match in. I never could believe a piano could burn like that, but it did."[5] As one critic wryly noted at the time, "Lewis makes parents mourn for the comparative quiet of Presley."[6]

Driven by his wild stage act, performed in cities across America, "Whole Lotta Shakin'" went to number one on both the country-and-western and the R&B charts (there were no rock-and-roll charts at that time). Yet for all of his popularity, audiences still expected Lewis to adhere to widely accepted social norms. So when the twenty-three-year-old piano pounder married his fourteen-year-old second cousin in 1958, many Americans were outraged. Although Lewis claimed that such a marriage was not unusual in the rural Louisiana region where he grew up, that explanation did not satisfy indignant Americans who believed that

Jerry Lee Lewis's wild onstage antics shocked observers, but their reaction paled in comparison to the public's outrage over his marriage to his fourteen-year-old second cousin.

the union was incestuous, and Lewis found his career sidetracked.

"Be-Bop-a-Lula"

Lewis was not the only performer whose antics in front of an audience gave him an almost-mythical status. Down the road in Nashville, Gene Vincent was gaining considerable attention for his hits, including "Be-Bop-a-Lula," "Race with the Devil," and "Crazy Legs." And Vincent's appearance foreshadowed the rock star image that would become commonplace in later

decades. He was the first rocker to dress from head to toe in black leather, he had a nasty limp that was a permanent legacy of a motorcycle accident, and he put forth a menacing swagger onstage while holding his mouth twisted into a sneer. Just as punk rockers would decades later, Vincent thrashed about while singing, leaping from amps and writhing on the stage on his back. Unfortunately, Vincent had a problem that would cut short his career: Because his leg had never healed properly and caused him considerable pain, he was addicted to painkillers and alcohol. This substance abuse caused him to experience wild mood swings and eventually killed him at the age of thirty-six.

Not every rock-and-roll star featured such an antisocial look, however. Vincent's rock-and-roll image stood in total contrast to the clean-cut Buddy Holly, whose trademark thick-framed glasses, skinny ties, and suit coats made him look more like a librarian than one of rockabilly's most talented singer-songwriters. But Holly's rhythm-heavy rock, catchy melodies, and teen-idol good looks propelled him to major stardom while he released a string of hit singles such as "That'll Be the Day," "Peggy Sue," "Not Fade Away," and "Rave On."

Little Richard and the Upsetters

Holly, like many early rock-and-roll musicians, was essentially interpreting black music for a white audience. But having been exposed to this music, white teenagers were also buying records by black artists in unprecedented numbers. Among African American musicians, no one delivered the frenzied, hard-charging sound of black rock and roll better than Little Richard Penniman.

Born in 1932, Little Richard got his start singing in the church choir as a child. But when he started to rock and roll with his band, the Upsetters, Little Richard did Jerry Lee Lewis one better, dressing in outrageously glitzy outfits,

Buddy Holly (right), shown here with his band the Crickets, is widely considered to be one of the greatest singer/songwriters in rock history.

wearing a tall pompadour hairdo, and lightening his face with makeup. As drummer Charles Conner later recalled, the band's name "wasn't just a name; when we'd go into a place, we'd upset it! We were the first band on the road to wear pancake makeup and eye shadow, have an earring hanging out of our ear and have our hair curled."[7]

During the highly conservative 1950s, Little Richard's barely concealed homosexuality was considered as bold as his music. Few teenagers seemed to know or care about his sexual orientation, however, and Little Richard's singles, such as "Long Tall Sally," "Slippin' and Slidin'," "Ready Teddy," and especially "Good Golly Miss Molly" and "Tutti Frutti," all released in the few years between 1955 and 1957, became instant rock classics.

Shrieking his trademark head-shaking "Whooo!" and hammering out the boogie-woogie rhythm on the piano, Little Richard added new vocabulary to teen slang when he howled the famous opening line to "Tutti Frutti": "Awhop-bob-a-Loo-Mop Alop-bam-boom!"[8]

Chuck Berry: The Rock-and-Roll Poet

Little Richard's brand of rock and roll came down to a driving beat and simple, suggestively catchy words. But right in the midst of this flamboyant rock rebellion a St. Louis hairdresser named Chuck Berry added an intellectual aspect to the music and, in doing so, became the first rock-and-roll poet.

Berry wrote songs about cars, boredom with high school, guitars, young love, and, of course, rock-and-roll music itself. In other words, every 1950s American teenager could relate to Berry's subject matter. He started each song with the same hot guitar lick that came to symbolize rock and roll in those early years. Onstage he would perform his famous duckwalk, loping along with one knee bent and the other leg out front pulling him across the stage, all the while strumming his guitar.

Berry's songs "Johnny B. Goode," "Maybellene," "Roll Over Beethoven," "Sweet Little Sixteen," "Memphis," and "Rock and Roll Music" shone with joyous—and smart—rock-and-roll poetry. In "Maybellene," for example, Berry sings about motivating over the hill when he sees Maybellene in a Coup de Ville. And although the Cadillac was rolling on the open road, nothing could outrun his big Ford. In "Roll Over Beethoven," Berry jokes about the popular cliché (at the time) that Beethoven would roll over in his grave if he heard rock and roll. Berry sings that his temperature's rising and the jukebox is blowing a fuse while his heart's beating out a rhythm and his soul is singing the blues. Finally, he instructs Beethoven to roll over and tell composer Tchaikovsky the news.

Berry's intelligent and intricate wordplay conveyed humorous stories that were unique in an era when rock-and-roll lyrics consisted of simple repetitive phrases such as "we're gonna rock around the clock tonight" or "rave on it's a crazy feeling."

The Rock-and-Roll Backlash

The suggestive lyrics and stage moves of Jerry Lee Lewis, Elvis Presley, and Little Richard drew scorn from national critics. In Anti-Rock, *Linda Martin and Kerry Segrave describe the rock-and-roll backlash.*

In April 1956 the mass circulation paper, the *New York Daily News,* ran a two-part series slamming rock as an "inciter of juvenile delinquency." . . . The series even then was predicting the death of rock mainly because "disgusted adults were battling the music of delinquents." According to the writer, Jess Stearn, it had taken a lot to set off this adult revolt, "riots and bloodshed, slurs on the national anthem, and slowly gathering public disgust at a barrage of primitive jungle-beat rhythms, which when set to lyrics at all, frequently sound off with double meaning leer-ics few adults would care to hear." . . .

The editors of *Music Journal* were much more horrified and revolted by the specter of rock and roll. The magazine considered it to be its "duty" to comment on "the most disgraceful blasphemy ever committed in the name of music." . . . The music was savage, illiterate, and vicious and the link between the music and juvenile delinquency was overwhelmingly clear. Teens listening to rock were [according to the magazine]

definitely influenced in their lawlessness by this throwback to jungle rhythms. Either it actually stirs them to orgies of sex and violence (as its model did for the savages themselves), or they use it as an excuse for the removal of all inhibitions and the complete disregard of the conventions of decency. . . . It has proved itself definitely a menace to youthful morals and an incitement to juvenile delinquency. . . . The daily papers provide sufficient proof of their existence. . . . It is . . . entirely correct to state that every proved delinquent had been definitely influenced by rock 'n' roll.

Chuck Berry wrote songs about subjects that every American teenager in the fifties could relate to, such as cars, young love, and rock music itself.

In December 2001 Berry recalled in an interview with *Rolling Stone* magazine that the key to his success was his concentration on the source of his money:

> I wrote about cars because half the people had cars, or wanted them. I wrote about love, because everybody wants that. I wrote songs white people could buy, because that's nine pennies out of every dime. That was my goal: to look at my bankbook and see a million dollars there.[9]

By 2001 Berry had little need to worry about money: He had made his million many times over. Yet when the original rock-and-roll poet was first singing his songs, success was not a sure thing. Indeed, rock and roll was falling on hard times because of a conservative social backlash and the pressure placed on its budding stars to succeed. The style would only be saved by a fresh infusion of talent—from across the Atlantic—thousands of miles away from the American South where the music was born.

Chapter Two

The Beatles and the British Invasion

At the beginning of the 1960s, rock-and-roll music was in sorry shape. The founding fathers of rock had been silenced: Elvis was drafted into the army in 1958, and that same year Little Richard found religion, renounced his rock-and-roll lifestyle, and quit the entertainment business to preach the gospel. Chuck Berry was imprisoned for transporting an underage girl across state lines (Berry claimed he was set up by police). And after Jerry Lee Lewis married his fourteen-year-old second cousin, he found it extremely difficult to find work as many Americans were repulsed by what they considered an incestuous union. Perhaps the most singular event that marked the end of the 1950s rock era occurred one night in February 1959 when an airplane carrying Buddy Holly and two other rock musicians, Richie Valens and J.P. Richardson, crashed into an Iowa cornfield, killing all three.

By 1960 rock and roll in its early, unpolished form had faded away. The new stars were clean-cut white teenage crooners such as Pat Boone, Fabian, Frankie Avalon, and Paul Anka. In fact, rock had been so sanitized by these innocuous teen idols that in 1962 Bing Crosby, one of the most popular singers from the World War II era claimed, "Rock 'n' Roll seems to have run its course. . . . [and will be replaced by] slow, pretty ballads."[10]

Crosby was hardly the first observer, nor would he be the last, to predict the death of rock. Music critics and authority figures had been making that prediction since Bill Haley rocked around the clock in 1954. What Crosby had no way of knowing was that while he was making his weighty pronouncement, a group of talented young men from Liverpool, England, was about to take the world by storm, enshrine rock music to a permanent place in history, and change the way people looked, talked, and even thought.

The band was the Beatles, and its members, guitarist John Lennon, bassist

Paul McCartney, lead guitar player George Harrison, and drummer Ringo Starr, were learning their craft playing the songs of Little Richard, Chuck Berry, the Everly Brothers, Gene Vincent, Buddy Holly, and other founding fathers of rock. But instead of copying the music directly, the Beatles put their own spin on the music, throwing in occasional jazz chords and singing with

California Surf Sounds

By 1962 California had surpassed New York as the most populous state in the nation, and the California lifestyle of sun, surf, and sand inspired a new sound called surf music. The man called "the King of the Surf Guitar" was Dick Dale, who used his Fender guitar and Fender Showman amp to produce twangy, reverb-heavy rapid-fire guitar licks reminiscent of ocean waves rolling over a surfer's head. Dale explains this concept in David P. Szatmary's Rockin' in Time: A Social History of Rock and Roll.

There was a tremendous amount of power I felt while surfing and that feeling of power was simply transferred into my guitar when I was playing surf music. The style of music I developed . . . was the feeling I got when I was out there on the waves. . . . Locked in a tube with the whitewater caving in over my head.

Dale's songs, such as "Let's Go Trippin'" and "Surfbeat," in-spired a wide range of imitators. But the most popular producers of California surf music were the Beach Boys (although only one member of the band actually surfed). The group's stellar four-part harmonies, sophisticated musical arrangements, and contagiously catchy songs, such as "Surfer Girl," "Fun, Fun, Fun," "California Girls," "Help Me Rhonda," and "I Get Around," all written by Beach Boy leader Brian Wilson, were number-one hits and would remain staples on oldies radio stations more than four decades after their release. The group moved beyond surf music, however, and in 1966 it released its masterpiece "Good Vibrations," which lasts three minutes and thirty-nine seconds and took six months to produce. The psychedelic sound put forth by this song was said to have in-spired the Beatles to make the groundbreaking Sgt. Pepper's Lonely Hearts Club Band.

an almost angelic three-part harmony that had previously been lacking in the performance of most rock songs. In addition to playing rock standards, Lennon and McCartney began writing their own music, which was unlike anything anyone had ever heard.

The Lads from Liverpool

Although the Beatles seemed like an overnight sensation when they became huge stars in the United States in 1964, Lennon, McCartney, and Harrison had actually been playing together for more than five years. Like millions of other teenagers, they had been strongly influenced by Elvis Presley after "Heartbreak Hotel" became a huge hit in Britain in 1956. As Lennon later commented, "Once I heard [Elvis] and got into it, that was life, there was no other thing. I thought of nothing else but rock 'n' roll."[11]

Accompanied by an ever-changing succession of drummers, Lennon, McCartney, and Harrison played in a group at first called the Quarry Men, then the Silver Beatles, and finally the Beatles. (In choosing that name for his band, Lennon was attempting to emulate the insect-based name of one of his favorite bands, Buddy Holly and the Crickets.)

The Beatles were hardly what could be called an instant success. In 1960 the band was booked into an extended engagement at a nightclub in the notorious red-light district of Hamburg, Germany, an area known as the Reeperbahn, which was filled with seedy music clubs, live sex shows, prostitutes, transvestites, and drunken sailors. There, fueled by amphetamines and beer, the Beatles played up to ten hours a night, seven days a week.

This apprenticeship proved valuable, however. To stave off boredom—and to please the rowdy crowds—the group began to experiment with new chords and to learn new songs. As Lennon later recalled, "In Hamburg we had to play for hours and hours on end. Every song lasted twenty minutes and had twenty solos in it. . . . That's what improved the playing. And the Germans like heavy rock, so you have to keep rocking all the time; that's how we got stomping."[12]

Although the early crowds consisted mostly of drunken sailors, gangsters, and prostitutes, the Beatles' exuberant music soon began to attract a crowd of sophisticated local art students and philosophers. One who came to hear the Beatles perform was Astrid Kirchherr, an artist, photographer, and fashion designer, and she helped make musical history. Kirchherr used her camera to record some of the earliest images of the Beatles as a group, and she talked the band into abandoning their greasy Elvis-style pompadours in favor of the "French cut" style, in which the hair was allowed to fall over the ears and was trimmed neatly all around, creating kind of a "moptop." At a time when men almost universally wore their hair trimmed short, the Beatles' new hairdo was considered a radical, even rebellious, look.

Beatlemania

Eventually, the Beatles returned to Liverpool, and their newly developed sound helped them land a gig playing daily lunch-hour shows at a basement club called the Cavern. Over the next several years, the Beatles attracted an ever-growing crowd of fourteen-year-old girls, office workers, and secretaries in short skirts and beehive hairdos who packed into the club during their lunch breaks. Some of these young women carried large purses with homemade embroidered messages that read "I Love You John," "I Love Paul," and "I Love the Beatles."[13]

Onstage, the band had an unusual stage presence. Instead of putting a professional face on their well-crafted music, they fooled around, eating lunch, smoking, and joking with each other and the audience between songs. John Lennon's boyhood friend, Pete Shotten, describes the band's quick-witted antics onstage:

The Beatles perform at the Cavern Club in Liverpool, England, in 1963.

John, with his lifelong inability to remember lyrics, often ended up ad-libbing the words to his favorite rock & roll classics, peppering the familiar melody with obscenities, in-jokes, and snatches of his inimitable gobbledegook. As often as not, the results singularly failed to fit the song's original meter, and the Beatles rendition would peter out in a chorus of laughter. . . . This evident spontaneity—coupled with the awesome firepower and tightness of the band when it did get down to business—perfectly complemented the primeval ambience of the place itself, and enabled the Beatles to regularly eclipse all other . . . bands who preceded or followed them onto the Cavern stage.[14]

In 1961, as the Beatles were endearing themselves to an expanding audience, they hooked up with Brian Epstein, a twenty-seven-year-old record store owner who became the band's manager. Although he was inexperienced as a promoter of musicians, Epstein propelled the Beatles toward stardom through sheer dogged determination. He made them clean up their act by giving up eating, smoking, and swearing onstage, and he dressed them in suits and ties. Meanwhile, band members began to write their own songs, which allowed them to showcase their talent individually. Lennon and McCartney were a particularly potent songwriting team, and

early songs such as "Love Me Do," "PS I Love You," and "Ask Me Why" were excellent vehicles for showcasing the band's tight vocal harmonies and instrumental talent during live performances.

The Beatles' obvious talent, coupled with Epstein's promotion, eventually caught the attention of a major record label. In August 1962 the Beatles were awarded a contract with Parlophone Records, a subsidiary of the prestigious EMI record company. Parlophone's in-house producer was George Martin, a classically trained pianist whose background was producing light orchestral music. With his scholarly understanding of 1960s recording equipment and his ability to write unique horn and string arrangements, Martin's musical influence combined with the talents of the Beatles themselves in an exceptional synergy that would change the sound of rock and roll.

Into the Top Twenty
By the autumn of 1962 "Love Me Do" was selling briskly in Liverpool, and those sales lifted the Beatles' first single into the British list of top-twenty hits. Martin suggested the Beatles follow their hit with a tune written by a professional songwriter. Lennon refused, however, insisting that the Beatles had plenty of original material from which to choose.

Martin acceded to Lennon's demands, and the Beatles recorded two Lennon/McCartney compositions,

Brian Epstein (left) became the Beatles' manager in 1961 and was instrumental in their rise to stardom. George Martin (right) became the band's producer and has been called the fifth Beatle.

"Please Please Me," and "From Me to You." Both rocketed to number one within days of their release. These hit singles were later included on the Beatles' first long-playing (LP) album, *Please Please Me,* recorded during a marathon ten-hour session on February 11, 1963.

The fourteen songs on *Please Please Me* were a combination of original and cover tunes (songs written by other people) that had been the core of the Beatles' stage act for several years. The band's talent was well displayed on the album. Classic rock-and-roll tunes, such as "I Saw Her Standing There," demonstrated the group's penchant for soaring three-part harmony, and "Do You Want to Know a Secret" showed that the group could put forth songs that even parents would love.

Upon its release, *Please Please Me* immediately went to the top of the LP charts, staying there a record-breaking twenty-nine weeks. Little more than a year after meeting Brian Epstein, the

Beatles had become the hottest act in the British Isles.

When the band's fourth single, "She Loves You," was released in August 1963, the "yeah, yeah, yeah" chorus had millions of young people singing along with "the Fab Four," and the Beatles' look was all the rage. By this time, nearly every schoolboy in Britain was cutting his hair in the moptop fashion of John, Paul, George, and Ringo. Stores that sold pointy ankle-high boots with stacked heels, or "Beatle boots," could not keep them in stock.

Americans Catch Beatlemania

The invasion of the United States by British rock and roll began in December 1963, when the Beatles released "I Want to Hold Your Hand" in Britain and the song quickly sold a million copies and went to number one. Days later, James Carroll, a disc jockey in Washington, D.C., played a copy of the record, which he had picked up overseas. Within minutes the station's phones began ringing nonstop with hundreds of requests for the song to be

On February 9, 1964, the Beatles performed on The Ed Sullivan Show *and as 73 million Americans watched, rock and roll entered a new era.*

A Hard Day's Night

During the Beatlemania era only three television networks operated in the United States, and the mass media was limited to broadcast television, radio, magazines, and newspapers. There was no MTV, Internet, twenty-four-hour entertainment networks, or any other way for Beatles fans to stay in touch with the band that they loved. So when the movie *A Hard Day's Night* premiered in June 1964, Beatles fans all over the world were able to get an inside look at their favorite band for the first time.

A Hard Day's Night opened in five hundred American movie theaters and grossed $1.3 million in its first week. More than a business success, the movie certified the Beatles as bona fide movie stars and added to their legend. The shots of the Beatles traveling, hanging around backstage, and answering fan mail in hotel rooms helped moviegoers bond with the band. It was also the first true music video ever filmed, with "jump cuts" of the band leaping through the air, running wildly across empty fields, playing live concerts before screaming audiences, and being chased through London's streets by teenage girls. The movie is now considered a classic, and even movie critic Roger Ebert used *A Hard Day's Night* to teach film classes, analyzing it for his students one shot at a time.

The movie showed that the Beatles were sweet, cute, funny, fashionable, and that they sang like angels. Lennon's irreverent wisecracks and antics demonstrated to fans that they too could rebel against the predictable, stale, and boring. A majority of the teens who watched the movie developed deep feelings of empathy—and love—for John, Paul, George, and Ringo.

played again. Other radio stations across the country obtained advance copies of the song from Capitol Records, and when it was released in the United States on December 25, it sold a million copies within days. One month later "She Loves You" was released, and it too went to number one on the *Billboard* charts, making it the first time any artist had produced two consecutive chart toppers.

When young Americans heard the Beatles and saw their pictures in national magazines, hysteria for the band, know as Beatlemania, broke out as quickly as it had in Britain. The band was booked to play on *The Ed Sullivan Show* for two consecutive weekends, February 9 and 16. The show received fifty thousand requests for tickets to the Beatles' performance in the seven-hundred-seat theater from which it was broadcast.

More than 73 million Americans—almost half the country—watched the Beatles on *The Ed Sullivan Show.* When the boys sang "Woooo!" and shook their long hair during "She Loves You," the teary-eyed teenage girls in the audience erupted in shrieks and screams that overwhelmed the sound system. By March, the Beatles had become the hottest band in America.

Searching for New Sounds

As the new kings of rock and roll, the Beatles' fame quickly spread around the world. Instead of sticking with the musical formula that won them success, however, the band continued to experiment musically. Still, the Beatles continued to please their listeners, releasing critically acclaimed, best-selling albums every year.

On *Rubber Soul,* the Beatles continued to reinvent their music, forging a dynamic blend of sweet acoustic guitars, jangling electric guitars, and lilting bass lines that were unique in pop music. Harrison added to the mix by playing a traditional Indian instrument known as a sitar on Lennon's "Norwegian Wood." This was the first time that the sitar was heard by most rock fans, but not the last. Soon dozens of other bands, including the Rolling Stones,

began to use the sound of the sitar layered within their rock songs.

The band's look evolved along with its music. When the Beatles began to use the psychedelic drug LSD in 1966, their appearance and music underwent another—this time mind-blowing—change. The cute moptops and Beatle boots of the early sixties gave way to shoulder-length hair, beards, beads, moccasins, sandals, and rainbow-colored clothing.

Two of the songs on their 1966 album *Revolver,* "She Said She Said" and "Yellow Submarine" were inspired by LSD trips. Lennon's acid-drenched vocals filled out such expansive songs as "I'm Only Sleeping" and "Tomorrow Never Knows," whose words were based on the Tibetan Book of the Dead, an ancient text that holy men read to the dying to help them on their journey through death and rebirth. No one had ever drawn on such heavy existential concepts for a rock song before.

Although they still recorded on four-track tape equipment that limited what could actually be heard on a record, the Beatles filled in songs with backward guitar licks, distortion, filters, and unconventional musical instruments. To get the bubbly sounds on "Yellow Submarine," Lennon blew through a straw in a glass of water. They added violins, cellos, trumpets, French horns, and other instruments traditionally used for performing classical music.

In order to elicit as many sounds as possible, Lennon piled sound over sound on the same small piece of recording

"Strawberry Fields Forever"

After the Beatles began experimenting with psychedelic drugs, their music underwent a noticeable change. Instead of producing three-minute pop songs—and recording them in a few days—the group began to spend months in the studio working on a single song, using unusual instruments and manipulating recording equipment in extraordinary ways. One of the first songs produced in this manner was "Strawberry Fields Forever," a whimsical and dreamlike Lennon composition that contrasts the unreality of the drug experience with childhood memories.

Producer George Martin framed "Strawberry Fields Forever" with tape loops and an extremely primitive electric synthesizer called a Mellotron and added a swirling "sound picture" marked by recordings of Ringo's drum cymbals played backwards. Martin, the band, and studio musicians also supplemented the sound with trumpets, cellos, and a harplike Indian instrument called a swordmandel played by Harrison.

In With a Little Help from My Friends: The Making of Sgt. Pepper, *Martin gives his opinion of the musical masterpiece:*

Way ahead of its time, strong, complicated both in concept and execution, highly original and quickly labelled "psychedelic," "Strawberry Fields Forever" was the work of an undoubted genius. We could not have produced a better prototype for the future. The care and attention we lavished on that track, its technical and musical excellence . . . we were all very proud of our new baby. For my money, it was the most original and inventive track to date in pop music.

"Strawberry Fields Forever" was released as a single in March 1967, with a short music video of the song (the first ever made).

tape. The rich aural effects of these "tape loops" would later be imitated during the 1970s by transistorized effects pedals and in the 1980s by digital computers, but in 1966, it was up to the Beatles to "invent" dozens of new sounds and present them to a waiting world.

Sgt. Pepper's Band

In 1967 the Beatles released the album *Sgt. Pepper's Lonely Hearts Club Band,* the first rock "concept" album—one in which all songs seem to be joined to one another. It was also one of the first albums to open to double size, and the first to have printed song lyrics.

The swirling psychedelic sounds on the album instantly became the soundtrack for the so-called Summer of Love, a time when long-haired hippies promoted the use of hallucinogenic drugs and held "love-ins" to promote world peace and the liberation of the human spirit from the confines of what they referred to as the "straight" world. As George Martin writes in *With a Little Help from My Friends: The Making of Sgt. Pepper,* "[*Sgt. Pepper* succeeded] in

The Beatles hold a copy of the Sergeant Pepper's Lonely Hearts Club Band, *album widely considered the first concept album in the history of rock and roll.*

Clearing the Mind
with Meditation

The success of *Sgt. Pepper* cemented the Beatles' reputation as the uncontested leader of the love generation. Band members were considered legends by their fans and were respected as artists by the establishment. They had more money and more fame than any rock band in history. But they were searching for something more.

After *Sgt. Pepper* was completed, Harrison's wife, Pattie, introduced her husband to Hindu mysticism as taught by the Maharishi Mahesh Yogi, who practiced transcendental meditation. In addition to meditation, Maharishi spread a message that sounded like lyrics to a Beatles song. He is quoted in *The Beatles Anthology* as saying, "Love is the sweet expression of life. It is the supreme content of life. Love is the force of life, powerful and sublime. The flower of life blooms in love and radiates love all around."

Taking the guru's message to heart, the Beatles learned meditation from him. Meditation involves clearing the mind of day-to-day thoughts by chanting a short phrase, called a mantra, over and over again. By practicing this technique only twenty minutes a day, people achieve extreme relaxation, creative inspiration, and mental clarity.

At that time, few people, especially in the United States, had heard of yoga or meditation, and like almost everything else that the Beatles tried, the fad of Indian mysticism quickly swept through the Western world. And this turn to Indian spirituality did wonders for the band. They all stopped taking drugs, as Lennon later explained in *The Beatles Anthology:* "If we'd met Maharishi before we had taken LSD, we wouldn't have needed to take it. . . . We don't regret having taken LSD. It was a stepping-stone. But now we should be able to experience things at first hand, instead of artificially with a wrong stepping-stone like drugs."

speaking for its age, capturing the sixties and much of what that era came to stand for in sound: the psychedelia, the fashions, the vogue for Eastern mysticism, the spirit of adventure, the whole peace and love thing, the anti-war movement; it was all there and more."[15]

After *Sgt. Pepper* the Beatles continued to set the trend for what music should sound like on the albums *Magical Mystery Tour, Beatles* (also known as *The White Album*), *Abbey Road,* and *Let It Be.* Instead of using their popularity for self-aggrandizement or to sell commercial products, however, they "sold" the message of peace and love to a generation hungry for a positive message. This was at a time when riots in inner-city neighborhoods, the Vietnam War, and antiwar protests were increasingly bloody and violent. And although they faced heavy criticism for their positions, they continued to produce music that was innovative, fresh, and new. Even after the group disbanded in 1970, John Lennon continued to risk his reputation and well-being to support the causes of peace and justice.

British Blues and Rock

The success of the Beatles in the United States during the midsixties paved the way for dozens of other British rock bands, such as the Rolling Stones, the Kinks, the Yardbirds, and the Who. As British rock promoter Arthur Howes comments, "The biggest thing the Beatles did was to open the American market to all British artists.

. . . Nobody had ever been able to get in before the Beatles. They alone did it."[16] Never before had the English so dominated the American record business.

Many of the groups who were part of this "British invasion" were strongly influenced by American music, specifically blues. Ironically, these British groups embraced black music with a much greater passion than bands in the United States, where the blues were born.

The most successful of the bands that followed the Beatles was the Rolling Stones, whose 1965 hit "(I Can't Get No) Satisfaction" landed the group a coveted gig on *The Ed Sullivan Show.* Whereas the Beatles had more of a folk music sound with soothing harmonies and mellow rhythms, the Stones took their cues from the blues music of Howlin' Wolf, Little Walter, Elmore James, and Muddy Waters, salting their songs with aggressive guitar licks and loud, driving rhythms. And whereas the Beatles, at least in the early years, were clean-cut and beloved by the parents of teens, the Stones, led by the strutting, sneering Mick Jagger, shocked adults with songs about casual drug use and careless sex.

The year that "Satisfaction" topped the charts, 1965, was the golden age of the British invasion. Some of the bands, such as Gerry and the Pacemakers and the Searchers, were colleagues of the Beatles from Liverpool. Other English bands, such as the Dave Clark Five, Herman's Hermits, the Mindbenders, and Manfred Mann, initially played the

The Rolling Stones perform at the Richmond Jazz festival in August 1964. The Stones, with their songs about drug abuse and casual sex, shocked adults.

same clubs as the Beatles. Although these bands were less than original, imitating the look and sound of the Beatles, their songs were well crafted and catchy, allowing them to top the charts, though not as often as the Fab Four.

Women, too, were part of the British invasion. Marianne Faithfull had a 1964 best seller with "As Tears Go By," written by Jagger and Rolling Stones' guitarist Keith Richards. During the later part of the sixties, Petula Clark had a string of hits, including "Downtown," "I Know a Place," and "Don't Sleep in the Subway," that featured memorable melodies and sing-along choruses.

Of all of the British invasion bands, perhaps the Who was the most unusual, and the band's antics during live performances alternately shocked and pleased the audiences. Onstage, the group performed its original songs, such as "Magic Bus" and "My Generation," with a punk attitude. Singer Roger Daltrey swung his microphone on its long wire in wide arcs, drummer Keith Moon savagely pounded his drum kit, and guitarist Pete Townsend leapt in the air and strummed his guitar with a stiff-armed windmill motion that led fans to first play "air guitar" in imitation. At the end of the evening Moon kicked over his drums as

Townsend rammed his guitar into the shredded speakers of his amplifier. Meanwhile, bassist John Entwistle stood almost comically stoic and silent holding down the rhythm in the midst of chaos.

By the late sixties British groups had gone psychedelic. Bands such as Cream, with Eric Clapton on lead guitar, combined the blues and jazz with drug-fueled jams that featured screaming lead guitar riffs, thundering

The Moody Blues

When the Beatles released *Sgt. Pepper* in 1967, the lush, swirling, orchestrated sounds of the dynamic album opened up a new chapter in rock-and-roll history that would be filled by bands that combined elements of classical music with rock beats, lyrics, and song structure. One of the first of these classical rock albums was *Days of Future Past* by the Moody Blues. This concept album featured the rock music of the Moody Blues combined with a full orchestra and depicted a typical day from morning to evening with musical interpretations of the sun coming up, a harried lunch hour, and the moon rising. The soothing psychedelic sounds of the album fit perfectly with counterculture hippie attitudes, and the singles "Nights in White Satin" and "Tuesday Afternoon" helped keep the album on the *Billboard* charts for more than two years.

The Moodys followed this success in 1968 with *On the Threshold of a Dream,* dropping the orchestra and instead using a Mellotron, a primitive type of synthesizer that produced sweeping orchestral sounds at the touch of a keyboard. On 1969's *In Search of the Lost Chord,* the band sang about psychedelic drug guru Timothy Leary in "Legend of a Mind" and the joys of transcendental meditation on "House of Four Doors" and "Om."

After releasing several more groundbreaking albums, the band started a five-year hiatus in 1972. The group united in 1977 and continued to tour and make records right through the end of the twentieth century. By 2002 the band had sold more than 60 million records, and all of its releases had reached into the upper regions of the top-forty charts. The Moody Blues retain a loyal following and are one of the top touring acts in history.

bass lines, and earth-shattering drum solos.

By the end of the sixties rock and roll had changed beyond recognition. The simple three-chord rockabilly of the fifties was ancient history as the Beatles inspired musicians to blast past old boundaries and search for new sounds. But the British were only part of the burgeoning musical scene during the sixties, and although many bands from across the Atlantic imitated rhythm and blues, a group of talented African American musicians in the American heartland had moved on, inventing a new kind of music that would prove to be as popular—and timeless—as the Beatles.

Chapter Three

Sweet Sixties Soul

While the Beatles dominated the rock charts during the midsixties, very few American acts were able to compete with John, Paul, George, and Ringo and the subsequent British invasion. Some of the few contenders who were able to challenge the Beatles were musicians and songwriters within the African American community who continued to create original and irresistibly danceable music.

Just as they had originated the sounds of rhythm and blues during the forties and rock and roll during the fifties, African Americans during the 1960s were developing the sounds of soul music, so-called because of its roots in spiritual gospel music. Soul music was modernized R&B, and the songs revolved around catchy melodies and a strong backbeat. Acts such as the Temptations, the Four Tops, and others featured lead vocalists whose tones dripped with a honeyed sweetness. Others, such as James Brown, Aretha Franklin, and Ray Charles sounded more like gospel singers who belted out soulful melodies guaranteed to command respect.

Soul music often featured tight background harmonies that utilized the gospel call-and-response technique, bobbing, weaving, and swirling around the lead vocals. Layered behind the catchy lyrics were short, tasteful saxophone riffs and an impeccable ringing rhythm section of jangling pianos, crisp staccato guitar chords, bouncing bass, chiming tambourine, and backbeat-heavy snare drums that made listeners want to snap their fingers, tap their feet, and dance.

But the importance of sixties soul went beyond just the music. Some of the soul groups, such as the Supremes, were nearly as popular as the Beatles, representing the first time that black artists had gained such widespread acceptance among white audiences.

Soul's rise came at a time when race relations in the United States were

Phil Spector's Wall of Sound

During the early sixties record producers held most of the power in the music studios. They chose the singers, picked the songs, and had the ultimate say on what a record would sound like. They also made most of the money. One of the most talented—and prominent—producers was Phil Spector, who worked with soul acts such as the Crystals, the Ronnettes, Ike and Tina Turner, and the Righteous Brothers.

Between 1962 and 1966 Spector produced a string of hits, including "Da Doo Ron Ron (When He Walked Me Home)" and "Then He Kissed Me" for the Crystals, "Be My Baby" for the Ronnettes, and "You've Lost That Lovin' Feeling" for the Righteous Brothers. These songs were produced using a now-famous recording technique that Spector called "the Wall of Sound."

To achieve the layered, dense, thunderous "teen symphonies" on primitive recording equipment, Spector packed his studio with dozens of musicians—three pianists, two drummers, two bass players, three sax players, and a five-piece string section. By repeated overdubbing, Spector produced a sound described on the Salon website:

The Wall of Sound was a musical mind-slam; it overloaded the auditory nerves with such sweepingly complex arrangements and such a barrage of instruments that it rendered the individual parts of the whole unrecognizable. Spector called his singles "little symphonies for the kids," but they were closer to opera—full of romantic [storm and stress] and more than occasional dips into absolute madness. The Wall was the sound of young love distilled into the three-minute opus—beautiful and horrible and sweet and suffocating.

To his towering layers of melody Spector piled on lyrics just a little more insistently than anybody else; he added singers whose voices could career from radio-ready fluff to an anguished wail on the turn of a note.

undergoing long-overdue changes. The glory days of soul music coincided with the passage of the Civil Rights Act in 1964 and the Voting Rights Act in 1965. These laws, enacted by Congress, allowed millions of southern blacks to vote for the first time and banned discrimination against African Americans in public places such as restaurants, hotels, bathrooms, libraries, and public transportation. This was also a time when Martin Luther King Jr. had become a household name and his speeches were inspiring millions of Americans, both black and white, to dream of a day when justice and equality would triumph over prejudice and discrimination. For many Americans, the soundtrack to this dream was provided by Smokey Robinson, the Supremes, Martha and the Vandellas, Stevie Wonder, Aretha Franklin, the Temptations, Marvin Gaye, Wilson Pickett, and many others.

The Soul Pioneer: Ray Charles

Soul music has its roots in the gospel sounds of the black church. For example, Ray Charles, one of the founding fathers of soul, was heavily influenced by the music he heard in church as a young boy in Greenville, Florida. As he once told interviewer Robert Palmer,

Greenville was a small town . . . and in the south, in those years, you went to church *every* Sunday. Whenever there was a revival meeting during the week, you went to that too. So naturally I

was around church music. The preacher would say a couple of lines and then the church would sing what he said. It was very ad-lib.[17]

Charles was born Ray Charles Robinson in 1930. He learned to play the piano at the age of five, but within a year he began to lose his eyesight. By the time he was seven, he was blind from glaucoma. Ray's mother enrolled him at the St. Augustine School for the Deaf and the Blind, where his musical talents were nurtured. He learned to read and write music in Braille, and he learned to play the saxophone, clarinet, and organ, while composing pieces for the school band on the piano.

Ray's mother died when he was fifteen, and he decided to quit school and pursue a musical career. He changed his name to Ray Charles to avoid being confused with the popular boxer Sugar Ray Robinson. At this time, Charles began his real-world musical education, playing in bands that performed blues, gospel, boogie-woogie, and jazz. He even gigged with an all-white hillbilly group for a time—highly unusual in the segregated South at that time.

By the 1950s Charles was writing his own songs, improvising blues lyrics over traditional gospel arrangements, and throwing in some rocking boogie-woogie flourishes on the keyboard. His talents were obvious to all who heard him, and Charles played and produced musical arrangements on million-selling blues records by Guitar Slim, whose titles, such as "You Reap What You Sow," were taken directly from gospel songs.

The melding of blues and gospel music was complete when, in 1953, Charles talked Jerry Wexler and Ahmet Ertegun, owners of Atlantic Records, into recording some of his original compositions. At a time when most singers were told by record producers what songs to play and how to play them, Charles insisted on total creative control. What Atlantic got by allowing Charles this musical freedom was a unique synthesis of gospel, blues, and rhythm and blues that was truly astounding, especially on the song "I Got a Woman," as Peter Guralnick writes in *The Rolling Stone Illustrated History of Rock:*

Ray Charles's unique blend of gospel, blues, rhythm and blues, jazz, and even country and western had made him a household name by 1959.

"I've Got a Woman," cut in Atlanta, was the consummate marriage of all the [musical] elements. . . . It featured, of course, [Charles's] strong gospel-based piano, a seven-piece group . . . that cooked, and a vocal which, in the studio version of the song, only begins to suggest the change that had taken place in Ray Charles; with a full-throated rasp, sudden swoops, falsetto shrieks and a sense of wild abandon, Charles totally removed himself from the polite music he had made in the past. There was an unrestrained exuberance to the new Ray Charles, a fierce earthiness that, while it would not have been unfamiliar to any follower of gospel music, was almost revolutionary in the world of pop.[18]

"I've Got a Woman," made Ray Charles a star, and the fiery soul sensation continued his success with a string of hits, including "Lonely Avenue," "This Little Girl of Mine," and "Nobody but You." On these records, to highlight the gospel feel, Charles added a three-woman vocal group, dubbed the Raelettes, to sing backup harmonies.

Throughout the fifties Charles continued to ingeniously synthesize musical styles, playing jazz, blues, old standards, and even country and western. Then, in 1959, Charles became a household name with the release of "What'd I Say." Guralnick analyzes the song, saying it features "a conventional enough blues riff with Latin rhythm and a gospel feel and six-and-a-half minutes of the most joyous celebration of utterly profane love. A kind of secular evocation of an actual church service, complete with moans, groans, and a congregation talking in tongues."[19]

"What'd I Say" sold a million copies, but it was too hot for some white-owned radio stations, which banned the record. And it was not just white people who condemned Charles, as he told Palmer:

I got a lot of criticism from [black] churches . . . and from musicians, too. They said I must be crazy and all that, and then, when they saw it was working, everybody started doing it. It's just like when a manager makes a business decision. If it works, he's a genius; if it doesn't he's a dog. Well, it worked, so I was a genius.[20]

Charles's musical genius allowed him to produce hits nearly every year of the 1960s, including "Georgia," "Hit the Road Jack," "Let's Go Get Stoned," and a deeply soulful reworking of the country song "I Can't Stop Loving You," which sold over 3 million copies. By the 1970s the founding father of soul was an international star, widely recognized for his musical contributions.

Sam Cooke

Whereas Charles was an electrifying singer, his rollicking shout lacked the smooth sweetness that would later

James Brown: Godfather of Soul

Singer James Brown has influenced dozens of soul acts since he first appeared on the scene during the late 1950s. His official website, James Brown: The Godfather of Soul, published the following biography of Brown.

He was born in South Carolina during the Great Depression. As a child, he picked cotton, danced for spare change and shined shoes. At 16, he landed in reform school for three years where he met Bobby Byrd, leader of a gospel group and life-long friend. . . .

After seeing Hank Ballard and Fats Domino in a blues revue, Byrd and Brown were lured into the realm of secular music. Naming their band the Flames, they formed a tightly knit ensemble of singers, dancers and multi-instrumentalists.

Over the years, while maintaining a grueling touring schedule, James Brown amassed 800 songs in his repertoire.

Mr. Brown became an icon of the music industry. With his signature one-three beat, James Brown directly influenced the evolutionary beat of soul music in the Sixties, funk music in the Seventies and rap music in the Eighties. . . .

With albums such as "Live at the Apollo," Mr. Brown captured the energy and hysteria generated by his live performances. People who had never seen him in person could hear and feel the excitement of him screaming and hollering until his back was soaking wet [with sweat]. . . .

As the leader of the James Brown Revue (The J.B.'s), James Brown sweated off up to seven pounds a night through captivating performances. His furious regimen of spins, drops, and shtick such as feigning a heart attack thrilled crowds. The ritual donning of capes and skintight rhythm & blues became part of his personal trademark as a performer.

come to be associated with soul music. That element was added by honey-voiced crooner Sam Cooke, whose vocal style would appeal to a large segment of the record-buying public.

Cooke, who was born in Chicago in 1931, spent his early career as the lead singer for the Soul Stirrers from 1951 to 1956. The six-man gospel group had been together, with a revolving cast of members, since 1930, but because of his great voice, Cooke was the band's first superstar.

As the Soul Stirrers toured black churches throughout the country, Cooke's handsome face and sweet tenor voice attracted an ever-growing crowd of teenagers, some of whom started Sam Cooke fan clubs. Singer Wilson Pickett commented on the overwhelming effect Cooke had on the young women, some of whom fainted when they heard the sweet gospel sounds he produced: "Them sisters fell like dominoes when Sam took the lead. . . . Bang. Flat-out. Piled three deep in the aisles."[21]

By 1957 Cooke was eager to throw off the musical and financial limitations imposed upon him by the gospel music establishment. He began to record for the musical mainstream and struck gold

James Brown (center), "The Godfather of Soul," jams with his band The Famous Flames in a recording session.

immediately with the release of "You Send Me," which rocketed to the top of the charts, selling 1.7 million copies within weeks.

The young man with the golden voice was signed to the prestigious RCA label in 1959, and he began writing and recording a string of hits that were instant classics, including "Chain Gang," "Wonderful World," "Bring It on Home to Me," and "Twistin' the Night Away."

In addition to adding an alluring new voice to the sounds of soul, Cooke revolutionized the business of music in the African American community. After seeing many black artists ripped off by white-owned record companies and denied royalties, or even the rights to their own songs, Cooke started his own publishing and management company, Kags Music. As the first black artist to accomplish this undertaking, Cooke leveraged this success into the formation of his own record company, Sar/Derby Records. This independent label specialized in turning gospel singers into pop stars. Some of the label's well-known names included Bobby Womack, Billy Preston, and Lou Rawls.

Cooke was at the top of his game on December 11, 1964, when he was shot by a Los Angeles motel manager during an argument. Cooke's funeral attracted thousands of hysterical mourners, some of whom were injured during the crush to see the soul singer for the last time. Two weeks later RCA released Cooke's final single, "A Change Is Gonna Come," a hauntingly beautiful last testament from a soul stirrer and a musical visionary.

Hitsville, U.S.A.

Sam Cooke's untimely death ended any chance that his publishing, recording, and management companies might have gone on to dominate the soul music business. Instead, that role fell to Berry Gordy, a former Ford auto worker who started Motown Records in a small bungalow on West Grand Boulevard in Detroit. Marked only by a sign that read "Hitsville, U.S.A.," this unassuming dwelling was ground zero for the Motown musical explosion that dominated the pop charts throughout the 1960s.

Gordy, born in Detroit in 1929, started writing songs as a teenager. In 1957 his first hit, "Reet Petite," was recorded by Jackie Wilson. The next year Gordy's song "Lonely Teardrops" was a million-selling hit for Wilson, although the songwriter himself received only one thousand dollars for his efforts. In 1959 Gordy borrowed eight hundred dollars from his parents and founded the Motown Record Corporation in the rented bungalow on West Grand. At the time his only ambition was to make enough money to buy the house, live upstairs, and keep a recording studio and office downstairs.

In its early days, Motown relied on other, larger record companies to promote and distribute its records. After achieving minor success with singles by a few R&B groups, Gordy released "Bad Girl," sung by Smokey Robinson and backed by a group called the Miracles. "Bad Girl" was distributed by Chess Records, but after the song reached number ninety-three on the national charts, Robinson convinced Gordy that Motown could make a lot more money if it distributed its own records. Against the advice of his lawyers, who warned that record distribution was too expensive an undertaking, Gordy pressed ahead and beat the odds with a number-two hit, "Shop Around," cowritten with Robinson and distributed by Motown.

Girl Groups

The late 1950s gave rise to the girl group fad, a wave of fascination for bands of female vocalists who produced an exhilarating mix of traditional pop, gospel-inspired doo-wop harmonies, and rhythm and blues. In The Rolling Stone Illustrated History of Rock, *Greil Marcus discusses girl groups:*

Of all the genres of rock & roll, girl-group rock is likely the warmest and the most affecting. . . . The form stretches from the classic broken hearts of the Chantels, the first major group, through Rosie and the Originals, the Shirelles, the Marvelettes. . . , Little Eva, [and] the Chiffons. . . .

Within that listing is emotion of staggering intensity, unforgettable melodies, great humor, a good deal of rage and a lot more struggle. . . . Still, it was music of celebration— of simple joy, of innocence, of sex, of life itself, at times—but most often it was a celebration of The Boy. The Boy is the central mythic figure in the lyrics of girl-group rock. He is shadowy: the boy who'll love walking in the rain, the fine fine boy, the leader of the pack, the angel baby. He is irresistible—and almost never macho. He is sensitive. He must be pursued. How to reach him? "You can call me up and have a date, any old time," grinned the Marvelettes [in the song] "Beechwood 4-5789." "I met him on a Sunday and my heart stood still," sang Darlene Love in the Crystals' magnificent "Da Doo Ron Ron." . . . The theme then, is little more than a variation on the Search for Perfect Love and the Attempt to Bring It Home to Meet Mom and Dad. . . .

The music was perhaps the most carefully, beautifully crafted in all of rock & roll.

Flush with success, Motown signed a number of female singers. Their resulting popularity would be a major part of what was known as the girl group style, in which young women harmonized on songs about love and their ideal boyfriends. Motown capitalized on this fad, charting hit after hit with Mary Wells ("Two Lovers," "My Guy") the Marvelettes ("Please, Mr. Postman"), and Martha and the Vandellas ("Heat Wave," "Dancing in the Streets").

"The Sound of Young America"

The success of Motown lay not only in the talents of its singers but also in its songwriters, particularly Lamont Dozier, who teamed up with brothers Brian and Eddie Holland. The so-called Holland-Dozier-Holland (H-D-H) team created an unprecedented line of immortal hits that would continue to achieve major airplay decades after their creation. A few of their many hits between 1964 and 1967 included "Baby I Need Your Loving," "I Can't Help Myself," "It's the Same Old Song," and "Reach Out, I'll Be There," for the Four Tops; "Can I Get a Witness" and "How Sweet It Is to Be Loved by You" for Marvin Gaye; "Heat Wave" and "Nowhere to Run" for Martha and the Vandellas; and their biggest-selling hits, "You Can't Hurry Love," "Baby Love," "Come See About Me," "Stop! In the Name of Love," "You Keep Me Hanging On," and "I Hear a Symphony" for the Supremes. In *The Rolling Stone Illustrated History*

of Rock Joe McEwan and Jim Miller explain the Holland-Dozier-Holland hit-making formula:

> As soul producers, they were little short of revolutionary. The trio rarely used standard song forms, opting instead for a simpler, more direct . . . pattern, anchored by an endless refrain of the song's hook line. The effect of this [circular] structure was cumulative, giving Holland-Dozier-Holland productions a compulsive momentum. [And] each and every one of them was immediately familiar, subtly distinctive and quite unforgettable. . . .
>
> Following Gordy's lead, Holland-Dozier-Holland exploited gospelish vocal gestures in a pop context, now defined by their own streamlined approach. If the vocalists provided emotion, the band mounted a nonstop percussive assault highlighted by a "hot" mix, with shrill, hissing cymbals and a booming bass—anything to make a song jump out of a car radio. With tambourines rattling to a blistering 4/4 beat, the H-D-H sound, introduced on "Heat Wave" and perfected on records like the Four Tops' "Reach Out, I'll Be There" and the Supremes' "You Can't Hurry Love" (both from 1966), came to epitomize what Motown would call "The Sound of Young America."[22]

The Motown Finishing School

Motown's joyous music helped make it one of the largest black-owned companies in the United States by the late 1960s. But talented songwriters and great production values were only part of the unbeatable Motown formula. Gordy's management company, International Talent Management (ITM), groomed the stars to play at the best nightclubs in America, many of which had been strictly off limits to black people before the civil rights era. Gordy felt that in order to present his acts to the widest audience, he needed to teach the singers, many of whom grew up poor in Detroit housing projects, how to project an image of elegance and grace. To facilitate this goal, ITM hired Maxine Powell, who owned a finishing and modeling school, to groom Motown artists. Powell later described her work:

The golden-voiced Sam Cooke started writing and recording a string of hits in 1959. Cooke's career was cut short when he was shot dead during an argument with a motel manager in 1964.

> The singers were raw. . . . They were from the streets, and like most of us who came out of the [housing] projects, they were a little crude: some were backward, some were arrogant. They had potential, but they were not unlike their friends in the ghetto. I always thought of our artists as diamonds in the rough who needed polishing. We were training them for Buckingham Palace and the White House, so I had my work cut out for me. . . . Many of them had abusive tones of voice, so I had to teach them how to speak in a nonthreatening manner. . . . Many of them slouched, so I had to show them what posture meant. Some were temperamental and moody; I would lecture them about their attitude. . . . I chose which clothes were best for them as well. We used to call them "uniforms." . . . As far as makeup, I worked with all of the girls on wigs, nails, and that sort of thing. And on stage technique, I taught them little things like never turning their backs to an audience,

Aretha Franklin Demands R-E-S-P-E-C-T

The civil rights movement of the early sixties gave a measure of political clout to African Americans for the first time during the twentieth century. As young African Americans flexed their new political muscle, several soul artists released songs such as James Brown's "Say It Loud, I'm Black and I'm Proud" (1969) and Marvin Gaye's "What's Goin' On" (1971), which acted as soundtracks to what came to be called the black power movement. But nothing grabbed the listener like Aretha Franklin spelling out R-E-S-P-E-C-T in her 1967 hit "Respect," as Gillian G. Gaar writes in She's a Rebel.

"**R**espect" hit a potent nerve in 1967. . . . Riots broke out in the black neighborhoods of several cities across America throughout the summer. . . . [As Phyl Garland wrote,] "Newspapers, periodicals and television commentators pondered the question of 'Why?' as Aretha Franklin spelled it all out in one word, R-E-S-P-E-C-T!". . . . *Ebony* writer David Llorens dubbed 1967 "the summer of 'Retha, Rap and Revolt!" But "Respect's" broad appeal was also due to the fact that the song could be read in a number of different ways. "It could be a racial situation, it could be a political situation, it could be just the man-woman situation," Tom Dowd, the recording engineer for the song, told *Rolling Stone*, adding, "Anybody could identify with it. It cut a lot of ground." . . .

"Respect" was followed into the Top 10 by . . . "(You Make Me Feel Like) A Natural Woman" and the LP *Aretha Arrives*. She began 1968 with a smash hit single and album, "Chain of Fools" . . . and *Lady Soul;* each went to number 2 in the charts. During the rest of '68 and '69 she would have eleven further Top 40 singles, three more Top 20 albums. . . and win the first two in a string of ten consecutive Grammy awards. . . .

By the end of the decade Aretha Franklin was clearly one of America's top female singers and an international star.

never protruding their buttocks onstage, never opening their mouths too wide to sing, how to be well-rounded professionals. I had to force these lessons. . . . The youngsters often had to be pushed and shoved. . . . We really wanted young blacks to understand that you do not have to look like you came out of the ghetto in order to be somebody other blacks and even whites would respect when you made it big.[23]

Gordy put the refined middle-American gloss on Motown artists during an era in which bloody inner-city riots and the rise of what was called the black power movement made many whites suspicious or even antagonistic toward any manifestation of African American culture.

Despite Gordy's best efforts to create a well-oiled soul music machine, there were cracks in Motown's veneer. The talented studio musicians who played on nearly every record—James Jamerson Sr. on bass, Benny Benjamin on drums, Joe Messina and Robert White on guitar, and James Giddons on percussion—were poorly paid and were unknown among the general public who adored the music. This led to great discontent behind the scenes.

In addition, Gordy tightly controlled what songs were written, who sang them, and when they would be released. Although often commercially successful, this stern creative control irked many of the stars who were the public face of Motown. And some of the song formulas were recycled endlessly by the same bands; thus, the catchy melody and beat of "Heat Wave" became "Quicksand," which morphed into the poor-selling "Live Wire." Despite these deficiencies, Motown hits blasted out of nearly every radio during the 1960s, and 75 percent of the company's records at least listed in the top one hundred on the national record charts. With their appealing melodies and irresistible rhythms, the sounds of Motown will forever remain an aural snapshot of the exciting sixties. But, along with Beatlemania and the British invasion, soul was only part of the complex and turbulent musical scene that dominated rock and roll during that era.

Chapter Four

Folk Rock Turns Psychedelic

During the 1960s rock-and-roll music underwent an unprecedented renaissance, led by the Beatles and African American soul singers. And while those artists dominated the charts for a time, a third strand of rock and roll competed successfully for the public's hearts and minds. Like soul, this music, known as folk rock, had roots deep in American history.

Folk rock's rise began in the early 1960s, with country and bluegrass musicians who had been blown off the stage during the fifties by rockabilly and rock and roll. These performers of traditional music found a new audience among white college students, and a movement, known as the folk revival, spurred a renewed interest in old-time bluegrass musicians such as mandolin player Bill Monroe, banjo picker Earl Scruggs, and flat-pick guitar wizard Doc Watson.

At the same time, a new generation of musicians, including Phil Ochs; Dave Van Ronk; Peter, Paul, and Mary; and Joan Baez were performing in clubs in New York City's Greenwich Village, reinterpreting traditional white country ballads and black blues music for a growing baby boomer audience. In *Song and Dance Man III* Michael Gray portrays the outlines of this music in his characterization of the folk group Peter, Paul, and Mary:

> To sound like a "folk singer" you were supposed to be smoothly [honest], Angry, and above all Sensitive. It is hard to pin down precise criteria but it's enough to say that Peter, Paul & Mary fitted the bill. With a name like that how could they fail? They were the Greenwich Village ideal—white, clean and middle-class.[24]

The Voice of a Generation

Although the music of artists like Peter, Paul, and Mary sounded contemporary, the subjects they sang about—indeed,

Woody Guthrie

Woody Guthrie had a profound influence on the American folk music movement, inspiring Bob Dylan to write protest songs. The following biography of Guthrie is from the website maintained by the Woody Guthrie Foundation and Archives:

Woodrow Wilson Guthrie was born on July 14, 1912, in Okemah, Oklahoma. . . . In 1931, when Okemah's boomtown period went bust, Woody left for Texas. . . . Due to the lack of work, and driven by a search for a better life, Woody headed west along with the mass migration of "dust bowl refugees" known as "Okies." These farmers and unemployed workers from Oklahoma, Kansas, Tennessee, and Georgia had also lost their homes and land, and so set out with their families in search of opportunities elsewhere. Moneyless and hungry, Woody hitchhiked, rode freight trains, and even walked to California, developing a love for traveling on the open road—a practice which he would repeat often.

By the time he arrived in California, in 1937, Woody had experienced the intense scorn, hatred, and antagonism of resident Californians who were opposed to the influx of outsiders. Woody's identification with outsider status would become part and parcel of his political and social positioning, one which gradually worked its way into his songwriting, as evident in his Dust Bowl Ballads such as I Ain't Got No Home, Goin' Down the Road Feelin' Bad, Talking Dust Bowl Blues, Tom Joad and Hard Travelin'. His 1937 radio broadcasts on KFVD, Los Angeles . . . brought Woody . . . wide public attention, while providing him with a forum from which he could develop his talent for controversial social commentary and criticism on topics ranging from corrupt politicians, lawyers, and businessmen to praising the humanist principles of Jesus Christ, Pretty Boy Floyd, and Union organizers.

the songs themselves—often dated back decades, if not longer. For example, many Greenwich Village folk singers were inspired by the music of Woody Guthrie, who had become well known after penning "This Land Is Your Land" during the early 1940s. Guthrie also wrote dozens of songs about government corruption, corporate greed, racism, and discrimination.

One of Guthrie's direct musical descendants was twenty-year-old Bob Dylan (born Robert Zimmerman), who idolized the folk singer. In 1961 Dylan hitchhiked from his hometown in Hibbing, Minnesota, to the New Jersey hospital where Guthrie lay dying, nearly paralyzed by Huntington's disease. After playing Guthrie a few of his protest songs and gaining the dying man's approval, Dylan joined the folk music scene in Greenwich Village.

Dylan imitated Guthrie, right down to the wool cap he wore and the ever-present cigarette dangling from his mouth. Dylan had another ambition, however—to write his own protest music combining country, folk, and blues. Most folk singers in the Village tried to imitate decades-old folk and blues music as precisely as possible, but the young man's nasal-inflected voice and intense, heartfelt music quickly gained recognition. Within a year Dylan was signed by the prestigious company

Woody Guthrie wrote dozens of songs about corporate greed, racism, discrimination, and government corruption.

Columbia Records for a five-album deal.

Although his first album, *Bob Dylan,* only had two original compositions on it, *The Freewheelin' Bob Dylan,* released in 1963, was laden with a form of protest music that no one had ever heard before. Whereas Guthrie had based most of his songs on traditional melodies and simple three-chord blues music, Dylan's songs, such as "Blowin' in the Wind" and "A Hard Rain's A-Gonna Fall," were intricate, wordy, and evoked surrealistic and sometimes harsh poetic images never before found in popular music. In the hands of other performers, Dylan's music had even more power. When Peter, Paul, and Mary performed "Blowin' in the Wind" at the 1963 civil rights march on Washington, it became a nearly instant anthem of the civil rights movement and soared to number one on the charts even before most people had heard of Dylan himself.

Dylan's impact on folk music became clearer still when *The Times They Are A-Changin'* was released in 1964. The album was filled with protest songs written in a style invented by Dylan. When the singer warned mothers, fathers, and senators that their children were beyond their command and that a cultural battle was about to shake their windows and rattle their walls on the

Bob Dylan, with his intricate, wordy songs that evoked surrealistic images, was called a genius by music critics.

album's title track, Dylan was branded a genius by critics, who called him the voice of the new generation. Dylan's most dedicated fans, as Gray writes, were "students and liberals who considered themselves radicals, hated pop music and wore Dylan on their sleeves like a political armband."[25]

Dylan Goes Electric

Not all of Dylan's innovations were instantly accepted by members of the folk music community or his fans. For example, many of Dylan's fans were aghast when, in 1965, he famously "went electric" with the release of *Bringing It All Back Home,* ripping into his songs with a Fender Stratocaster in hand and backed by a jangling rock ensemble. Meanwhile, Dylan's bitingly satirical and humorous side came to the fore with hilarious wordplay on songs such as "Subterranean Homesick Blues" and "Bob Dylan's 115th Dream." Although many hauntingly beautiful acoustic songs fill the album, such as the classics "Mr. Tambourine Man," "Gates of Eden," and "(It's All over Now) Baby Blue," many fans refused to accept the new Dylan sound.

Dylan's fans believed, as Gray writes, "here was this folk singer committing the ultimate sacrilege of singing rock 'n' roll songs with electric guitars behind him. Students—serious-minded young people unaware of the social upheavals about to happen—were appalled that Dylan should resort to such triviality."[26] When Dylan played songs from the album at the Newport (Rhode Island) Folk Festival, he was loudly booed, organizers threatened to unplug his amp, and he came back for an encore chastened, with his acoustic guitar in hand.

Dylan, only recently the golden boy of the folk scene, was angry. His next album, *Highway 61 Revisited,* reflected that anger in songs such as "Positively 4th Street," in which listeners heard Dylan castigating his critics, telling them that they had a lot of nerve, they were

insincere, and, in fact, Dylan thought they were a drag to be around. However harsh the singer's words might have been, the song became a staple on rock radio and would remain so for decades. The album also included the classic "Like a Rolling Stone," which at more than six minutes was (at the time) the longest song ever released on a 45 rpm single and the first to break the three-minute "barrier" to which radio programmers traditionally adhered.

Dylan's next album was a double-record set, *Blonde on Blonde,* which brought his album total to eight sides of vinyl in two years. This masterpiece contained another round of classics that for many listeners would still sound fresh in the next century. By this time, the singer had met his future wife, Sarah Lowdens, and love songs such as "I Want You," "Sad Eyed Lady of the Lowlands," and "Just Like a Woman," permeated the album between hallucinatory masterpieces such as "Visions of Johanna" and "Stuck Inside of Mobile with the Memphis Blues Again." On "Rainy Day Women twelve and 35," Dylan sang that everyone must get stoned, and the song was either one of the first pro-drug songs of the sixties or a commentary about the verbal stones hurled by his critics.

Dylan toured the world in 1965 and 1966, singing the songs that were the product of his recent burst of creativity. Backed by the electric group known simply as the Band, Dylan was booed by some, adulated as a rock god by others, and incessantly hounded by the press, which kept pinning the protest-singer label on him long after he had moved on musically. Parts of the tour were captured in the critically acclaimed film *Don't Look Back*.

Musically, Dylan refused to stand still. Ever the contrarian, Dylan would "go country" during the late sixties, releasing albums such as *Nashville Skyline* during the height of the electric psychedelic era. The singer had grown up on the honky-tonk music of Hank Williams and the rock and roll of Elvis Presley and Little Richard. In fact, he was quoted in his high-school yearbook as saying that he wanted to "join the band of Little Richard"[27] after graduation. He would re-

gain his title as the premier rock poet once again during the 1970s with a stellar series of albums including *Blood on the Tracks, Desire,* and *Street Legal.* And he would alienate even his most dedicated fans by becoming a born-again Christian during the 1980s. Although there was never a shortage of criticism and scorn during every phase of Dylan's career, he continued to make original, creative, and poetic music well into the twenty-first century. In February 2002 Dylan's forty-third album, *Love and Theft,* was hailed as a masterpiece by critics and won a Grammy (his seventh) for Album of the Year. And this time, the then-sixty-year-old Dylan had been

The Byrds combined folk music and rock to create a new genre called folk rock.

constantly playing concerts across the globe for more than fourteen years on what he jokingly calls his "Never-Ending Tour."[28]

Over the course of more than forty years, Bob Dylan would serve as a living illustration of how rock and roll could be an ever-changing, looping musical form capable of being shaped and reshaped to suit the performer's mood. Ironically, although critics had howled when Dylan went electric on *Bringing It All Back Home,* the rock band the Byrds had a number-one hit when they electrified "Mr. Tambourine Man," one of the acoustic numbers from Dylan's album. With angelic three-part harmonies spinning Dylan's dreamlike words, "Mr. Tambourine Man" combined folk and rock music so well that "folk rock" became an instant genre, practically overnight. In *The Rolling Stone Illustrated History of Rock,* Bud Scoppa writes, "The jaggedly beautiful sounds of [the Byrds'] twelve-string electric guitars was said to have a 'jingle-jangle,' after the line in the Dylan-penned song."[29]

The Jingle Jangle of Folk Rock

The fresh sound of the Byrds was a result of their personnel, who were folk singers and country musicians who shared a common interest in trying to emulate the sound—and the success—of the Beatles. As the Byrds' founder, Roger McGuinn, later stated, "The Beatles came out and changed the whole game for me. . . . I saw a defi-nite niche where the folk sensibility and rock-'n'-roll energy blended together. If you took John Lennon and Bob Dylan and mixed them together, that was something that hadn't been done before."[30] *Newsweek* magazine summed the new sound up in less detail, calling the Byrds "Dylanized Beatles [and] Beatlized Dylans."[31]

However it was defined, folk rock was seized upon by several groups looking to combine the personally expressive words of Dylan with the bright guitar and harmony work of the Beatles. And most of the bands that were successful at this brought something of their own creative inspiration into the music. The Mamas and Papas were one such group. This foursome of folk rock superstars produced a string of hit singles, including "California Dreamin'," "Monday Monday," and the autobiographical "Creeque Alley." This group was powered by "Papa" John Phillips's excellent songwriting with irresistible melodies soaring into the highest vocal range on the band's almost impossibly tight harmonies.

There were other stars of the folk rock movement, including Buffalo Springfield, the Lovin' Spoonful, the Turtles, Donovan, Simon and Garfunkel, and even Sonny and Cher. Although the popularity of some, such as Simon and Garfunkel, would last for decades, the folk rock boom itself did not last for more than two years. In the dynamic and exciting 1960s, change was constant. By 1967 millions of American youth were experimenting

Gram Parsons and Country Rock

Although Bob Dylan was the father of folk rock, he also triggered another musical style—country rock—when he combined his trademark storytelling lyrics with simple old-time country music backing. On his 1968 album *Nashville Skyline,* Dylan used country arrangements on songs such as "Lay Lady Lay" that included a pedal steel and flat-picking guitar played by some of Nashville's finest studio musicians.

Just as the Byrds had followed Dylan into folk rock, they experimented with country rock as well. Their 1968 album *Sweetheart of the Rodeo* featured banjos, pedal steels, and mandolins playing true-to-style bluegrass and honky-tonk arrangements. In addition to covering country standards such as "I Am a Pilgrim" and "You Don't Miss Your Water," the Byrds played original country rock songs written by eighteen-year-old Gram Parsons, who had recently joined the group.

Parsons was a leading proponent of country rock, a term he disliked, preferring instead *American cosmic music.* Parsons left the Byrds after *Sweetheart of the Rodeo* and formed the Flying Burrito Brothers, another extremely influential country rock group. Soon he moved on again, spending time with the Rolling Stones, inspiring that British rock group to write such country-flavored numbers as "Honky Tonk Woman," "Country Honk," "Dead Flowers," and "Wild Horses."

Parsons released two well-received solo albums—*GP* and *Return of the Grievous Angel*—during the early seventies. He was backed by members of Elvis Presley's band, many of whom had deep country roots. Parsons also discovered Emmylou Harris singing in a bar, and her soaring, ethereal harmonies may be heard on Parson's solo albums.

Parsons died of a drug overdose in 1973 at the age of twenty-six, but his influence was widely felt in the music of Elvis Costello, U2, Marty Stuart, Black Crowes, the Lemonheads, Nick Lowe, Uncle Tupelo, Son Volt, Tom Petty, and the Eagles.

with marijuana and the powerful hallucinogenic drug LSD, or acid. For musicians, acid would power a psychedelic revolution that would forever change the sound of rock.

The Byrds foreshadowed the new sound with the release of "Eight Miles High" in 1966. This song was yet another hybrid, combining a droning rhythmic beat, languid vocals, and a guitar solo inspired by the jazz giant saxophonist John Coltrane. As the first example of what would later be known as acid rock, this song was banned on many radio stations for its supposed references to drug use, although McGuinn claimed the song was about flying in a jet airliner eight miles above the earth.

San Francisco Psychedelia

For all of the change rock had seen, the one constant was its status as a means of expressing dissatisfaction with the status quo. By 1967 America was in the midst of a social upheaval that came to be called the hippie, or counterculture, movement. As a way of rejecting their parents' "straight" culture and protesting military involvement in Vietnam, millions of male baby boomers grew long hair and beards, and both sexes donned brightly colored tie-dyed clothes, sandals, and love beads. In *20 Years of Rolling Stone: What a Long, Strange Trip It's Been,* singer-songwriter David Crosby, formerly of the Byrds, observed at the time that the parents of baby boomers had little chance of stemming the counterculture movement:

On one side you got war; degradation, death, submission, guilt, fear, competition; and on the other hand you got a bunch of people lyin' out on the beach, walking around in the sun, laughin', playin' music, makin' love and gettin' high, singin', dancin', wearin' bright colors, tellin' stories, livin' pretty easy. You offer that alternative to a kid, man, and the kid ain't crazy yet. I think that they've probably lost the majority of their kids by now.[32]

At the epicenter of the hippie movement was the Haight-Ashbury neighborhood in San Francisco, a run-down area where affordable apartments butted up against the paradisiacal Golden Gate Park. Fueled by marijuana, acid, hallucinogenic mushrooms, and peyote buttons, several San Francisco bands emerged in Haight-Ashbury during the midsixties that made the pre-psychedelic Beatles look quaint, tame, and old-fashioned by comparison. Like many rockers of the 1960s, these musicians had roots in folk music. For example, Jerry Garcia, the lead guitarist of the Grateful Dead, had originally been a banjo player whose repertoire included many traditional old-time country songs. Paul Kantner, the founder of Jefferson Airplane, was a regular at San Francisco sing-along parties called hootenannies. Another Airplane member, Marty Balin owned the Matrix, a nightclub that featured folk music.

The Grateful Dead fused country, jazz, blues, folk, and bluegrass to form a new brand of music some critics referred to as acid jazz.

The Grateful Dead's Molecular Evolution

The folk scene, however, changed drastically in 1965 when novelist and acid guru Ken Kesey began to hold "acid tests," in which LSD—which was still legal at that time—was given to thousands at huge parties where people decorated their bodies with Day-Glo paint, watched protoplasmic light shows, and danced all night long to the psychedelic rock of the Grateful Dead. Kesey's acid tests spread LSD use far and wide, and the psychedelic revolution quickly overtook America. Garcia describes his reasons for partaking: "To get really high is to forget yourself. . . . And to

forget yourself is to see everything else. And to see everything else is to become an understanding molecule in evolution, a conscious tool in the universe."[33]

As the "house band" for the acid tests, the Dead fused country, blues, jazz, and bluegrass on electric instruments and formed a new brand of music sometimes called acid jazz because it relies on the improvisation and free-form expression found in jazz music. Social critic Charles Perry comments on this new sound:

> Most of the rock musicians in San Francisco were basically folkies learning how to play

The Doors Light a Fire

Sixties rock and roll was revolutionary music, and few musicians upset the social order with more relish than Jim Morrison, lead singer for the Doors. Morrison was fascinated by fire, surrealistic experiences, and exploring the depths of human consciousness. These themes were explored in songs such as the multimillion-selling "Light My Fire," "Strange Days," "Moonlight Drive," and "Break on Through." And with his tight leather pants, mop of wavy hair, and movie-idol good looks, Morrison was the prototypical rock star.

Morrison pioneered extreme rock star behavior as well, appearing on stage violently drunk while alternately insulting audiences and inciting them to riot and revolt. As Doors keyboardist Ray Manzarek is quoted as saying in David P. Szatmary's *Rockin' in Time: A Social History of Rock and Roll,* Morrison was interested in "anything about revolt, disorder, chaos. It seemed [to him] to be the road towards freedom—external revolt is a way to bring about internal freedom."

Morrison died in 1971, little more than half a year after Jimi Hendrix and Janis Joplin. Although the music of the Doors retains a fundamental grip on the play lists of modern radio stations, the group represented a wild, free, and often frightening aspect of the decade of protest and youth revolution.

electrified instruments. . . . They had a tentative sound at first and played a lot of solemn, chiming chords on the beat. When it came time for the guitarist to take a solo break, he often noodled up and down the notes of the scale in a way that might owe as much to inexperience in improvisation as it did to the influence of Indian ragas [traditional melodies].[34]

The music may have been tentative at first, but the Grateful Dead went on to record classic albums that mixed acid rock with jazzy folk overtones. Although their first albums, *Anthem of the Sun* and *Aoxomoxoa,* are psychedelic masterpieces, later records, such as *Workingman's Dead* and *American Beauty,* are loaded with folky three-part harmonies, ringing acoustic guitars, and understated leads by Garcia. Like most San Francisco bands, however, the Dead could best be appreciated live, and they themselves admit that they never captured their sound on records. As a result, the Dead toured relentlessly for nearly thirty years, keeping the counterculture movement of the 1960s alive among hundreds of thousands of dedicated fans until the death of Garcia in 1995.

Meanwhile, the careers of other San Francisco bands burned hot and fast. Jefferson Airplane was one of the first Bay Area bands to sign a major recording deal and the first to have a string of number-one hits. When the band released the album *Surrealistic Pillow* in 1967, music fans across the globe were able to hear the encapsulated San Francisco sound on songs such as "Somebody to Love" and "White Rabbit," a song based on *Alice in Wonderland,* and which has references to pills, mushrooms, and dreamlike experiences. Airplane lead singer Grace Slick was the queen of the psychedelic sound with her indomitable vibrato vocals swooping and soaring together with Kantner's perfect harmonies riding above the thundering bass of Jack Cassady and the screaming lead guitar of Jorma Koukonen.

The Blues Go Psychedelic
The folk-inspired psychedelic music played by groups like the Dead and Jefferson Airplane was but one part of the San Francisco sound. Other performers hearkened back to rock and roll's blues roots. Janis Joplin, who was strongly influenced by female blues singer Odetta and blues heavyweight Lead-

belly, was the best known of the San Francisco–based performers who drew heavily on rock and roll's blues heritage. After joining a band called Big Brother and the Holding Company in 1966, Joplin became a star almost instantly. Joplin was famous for wailing out songs such as "Piece of My Heart" and "Ball and Chain" with eyes closed, face contorted with pain, clutching a microphone in one hand and a bottle of Southern Comfort whiskey in the other. She shrieked, moaned, cried, screamed, and pounded her feet, lost in a world of her own as she sang for thousands of people. Joplin's music could not exactly be called blues, nor was it acid rock; hers was a sound the drunken singer jokingly called "alkydelic."[35] Joplin's blues came from her sad, lonely soul, and she barely lived to see the end of the sixties, dying of a heroin overdose on October 4, 1970, at the age of twenty-seven, barely four years into a meteoric musical career.

The Hendrix Experience
Whereas Joplin was influenced by the gruff and growling vocal styles of blues singers, psychedelic pioneer Jimi Hendrix took inspiration from the soulful riffs played by blues guitar players. Hendrix, born in Seattle in 1942, has often been labeled by critics as the greatest guitarist of the twentieth century, and few dispute that claim. He began his career by backing blues and soul artists such as B.B. King, Tina Turner, and Wilson Pickett. But Hendrix started his own

Janis Joplin, who sang the blues in a style she called alkydelic, *died of a heroin overdose in October 1970.*

group during the midsixties and soon moved to England, where he put together the Jimi Hendrix Experience with drummer Mitch Mitchell and bassist Noel Redding. The left-handed Hendrix played his Stratocaster guitar upside down and was able to create unearthly sounds that humbled established stars such as Pete Townsend and Eric Clapton.

Hendrix was unknown in America until 1967, when he played at the Monterey (California) Pop Festival. Dressed in buckles, beads, and feather boas, Hendrix stood in front of the mesmerized crowd playing guitar with his teeth. The wall of Marshall ampli-

fiers behind him shrieked with feedback as he put his fuzz tone, wa-wa, and phase effect pedals to the test. As the entire stage groaned and vibrated with the convoluted cascade of Hendrix's lead notes during "Wild Thing," the guitarist bent over, soaked his beloved guitar in lighter fluid, and lit it on fire. By the time the movie chronicling that performance, *Monterey Pop,* was released later that year, Hendrix was a guitar superstar, and anyone who heard him knew that rock and roll would never be the same as a result of his influence.

Hendrix released an incredible three albums in two years: *Have You*

Ever Been Experienced?, Axis-Bold as Love, and the double-album *Electric Lady Land.* Songs such as "Purple Haze," "And the Wind Cries Mary," "Little Wing," and his version of the Dylan song "All Along the Watchtower" became instant radio staples. Then, in September 1970, it all came crashing down. A drunken Hendrix accidentally overdosed on sleeping pills and died just two months short of his twenty-eighth birthday.

Although Hendrix's career was cut short, the fuzz-induced frenzy of his guitar work was imitated by a million guitar players, and a new genre—heavy metal—grew up directly from his flying fingers. He changed what it meant to be a lead guitarist, and though many would try, few would have the talent or free spirit to match Hendrix's technical or creative virtuosity.

The year 1970 was a watershed year for rock music. The Beatles broke up in April, and the deaths of

Jimi Hendrix plays at the Isle of Wight Festival in August of 1970. Some music critics have called Hendrix the greatest guitarist of the twentieth century.

Jimi Hendrix, Doors lead singer Jim Morrison, and Janis Joplin extinguished some of the leading lights of music. The decade had started out with earnest white folk singers trying to infuse rock and roll with importance and meaning; as the years proceeded, several new genres had been invented that would resonate through the music world for decades to come.

In ten short years the three-chord rock of Chuck Berry and Elvis Presley had been reshaped into sweet soul music, angry songs of protest, surrealistic dreamscapes of sound, and a heavy metal blues fury. The notes played and the words written during that decade changed the world, and they would continue to influence rock musicians well into the twenty-first century.

Chapter Five

Rock-and-Roll Superstars

D uring the 1960s the success of the Beatles, Bob Dylan, and various other stars made rock musicians some of the best-known celebrities on the planet—as instantly recognizable as national political leaders. Not only was their behavior and dress widely imitated, but these talented musicians generated billions of dollars by writing songs, making records, and performing. In fact, a new term was coined—*superstar*—to describe musicians who had succeeded far beyond the reach of stars in earlier years. It is little wonder then, as the seventies and eighties progressed, that rock star celebrity would sometimes take on more importance than the music itself. And that those who wanted to become superstars would be willing to do just about anything to attain that dream.

This idea was not in evidence, however, in August 1969, when, at the peak of the counterculture revolution, almost half a million people gathered in a field near Bethel, New York, to attend a rock-and-roll show. The three-day concert, officially known as the Woodstock Arts and Crafts Festival, featured twenty-seven popular musical acts, including the Grateful Dead; Janis Joplin; the Who; Jefferson Airplane; Crosby, Stills, Nash, and Young; and Jimi Hendrix. Although the promoters originally hoped that fifty thousand people would attend the concert, no one was prepared for the teeming throngs that made their way to Woodstock. There was not enough food, water, or bathrooms for the huge crowds, the New York State Throughway was closed because of the traffic, and severe rainstorms turned the concert site into a quagmire. Despite the hardships, there was little in the way of violence or crime. As the promoters boasted, with kids running the show, it was simply three days of peace, love, and music.

The youthful organizers of Woodstock might have seen the show's success in such idealistic terms, but record

In August of 1969, half a million rock and roll fans gathered near Bethel, New York, for the Woodstock Arts and Crafts Festival.

executives saw gold in those New York hills. The music business had grown steadily throughout the sixties, thanks to many of the performers featured at Woodstock, but still it seemed that the record companies had underestimated the mass attraction of rock-and-roll music.

Whereas rock and roll was once seen as a form of protest, following Woodstock many record company executives and musicians took a sharp turn away from the idealistic and moved rapidly toward the capitalistic, asking themselves why they were fighting a system that could reward them so well. This contradiction is explored by Ken Tucker in *Rock of Ages: The Rolling Stone History of Rock:*

> In the previous decade, rock was the stuff of the counterculture; in the 1970s . . . this music was the culture. In the 1960s, the music's authenticity was measured by the distance it placed between its re-

bellious, unkempt, [challenging] point of view and the [accepting], mannerly, tame world of professional entertainment. In the 1970s, this notion gradually came to be viewed as unrealistic and immature. For some longtime rock fans, this was proof positive that rock was no longer any good, that it had sold out and become family entertainment. . . . For others, though, it suggested the enormous outreach and ambition of the music. For the first time in its history, large numbers of people began to think that maybe rock and roll really was here to stay; that it could grow and become an artistic medium that could adapt to its aging audience as well as continue to attract the young fans who would remain the lifeblood of the music. What some saw as the death of rock as a challenging, creative medium, others recognized as an opportunity to spread the music's diverse messages to an unprecedented number of people. And, in some cases, to get rich while doing it.[36]

The Woodstock Effect

One of the first groups to benefit from this new view of rock and roll was Crosby, Stills, Nash, and Young (CSN&Y). When these musicians put their incredible harmonies and songwriting skills together, they became one of the first supergroups of the seventies. When CSN&Y performed at Woodstock, it was only their first gig, and they were terrified. But David Crosby, Steven Stills, Gram Nash, and Neil Young were veterans of sixties rock. Nash had several hits, such as "Bus Stop" and "Carrie Ann" with the Hollies, an English group that had ridden the wave of the Beatles-led British invasion. Crosby had served in the Byrds, and Stills and Young had played in the groundbreaking sixties band Buffalo Springfield.

The band's appearance at Woodstock, along with its heart-warming performance in the movie *Woodstock* released later that year, helped make its first album, *Crosby, Stills, and Nash* (made without Young), an instant best-seller. Although the group's sound was sort of psychedelic folk and seemingly unlikely to engender Beatlemania-like hysteria, the star status of band members allowed them to pack large sports stadiums throughout the early seventies—a feat previously reserved mainly for such huge bands as the Beatles and the Rolling Stones.

Music as Product

Crosby, Stills, Nash, and Young made history in another way. When their 1970 album, *Déjà Vu,* sold several million copies upon release, it established a standard by which record sales would be measured from then on. During the fifties and sixties, a record or album that sold half a million copies was considered a massive success and was referred to as a gold record. After Woodstock, the threshold was raised dramatically, and popular records were expected to go "platinum" by selling a million copies or "multiplantinum," with multimillions of copies sold.

Spurred on by these lucrative sales, the record business began a steady expansion, growing 25 percent a year during the early seventies. This in turn attracted the interest of huge multinational corporations, which purchased the record companies but had little interest in the high ideals of musicians' or in rock and roll as art form. By the mid-seventies, music was known within the record industry as "product," something to be labeled, put in a carton, and sold as quickly as possible, like a can of tuna, a bar of soap, or a bottle of soda.

The new attitude quickly fed back into the way musicians were viewed and promoted. Record executives realized they could reach more consumers if they divided up the music into neat categories and marketed it to specific "demographic" groups, such as older baby boomers, teenagers, and college students. Whereas baby boomers might like the mellow sounds of Crosby, Stills, and Nash, teenagers would be interested in the new heavy metal of Led Zeppelin, and college students could appreciate "art rock" by bands such as Yes and Pink Floyd. Later in the decade, as rock music fragmented to reflect audience demographics, disco, reggae, and punk would enter into this formula as well.

Radio programmers also followed this trend. As Tucker writes, during the seventies the "notion of *formatting,* of programming a certain kind of music for a certain segment of the audience to sell a certain kind of product, became the prevailing practice. . . . The idea was to attract the ideal demographic group for advertisers— [mainly] white teenagers with [allowances] to burn."[37]

Roll Over Beethoven

Radio programmers used polls, surveys, and focus groups to determine the type of music their listeners most wanted to hear. What they found in the post-Beatles era was that listeners' tastes in general had become more sophisticated, especially those in the high-school and college-age categories, desirable for the money they had available for spending. These people preferred music that was not available on short-playing singles. This led to the development of a new radio format known as album-oriented rock (AOR). At the same time, the overall quality of radio sound improved, especially on the FM band, which could broadcast in stereo, greatly enhancing the listening experience.

The main beneficiaries of these twin trends were English rock bands; as a result, the early seventies was a golden age for English rock. Inspired by the artistic works on the Beatles' *Sgt. Pepper* album, a new wave of British bands began to combine classically inspired orchestral music and rock and roll into

Fleetwood Mac's Classic Pop

Fleetwood Mac epitomized the sound of rock during the mid-1970s. Rollingstone.com has the following biography of the band:

One of the most commercially successful rock groups of all time, Fleetwood Mac was formed in London in 1967 by ex-members of John Mayall's Bluesbreakers: Mick Fleetwood (drums), John McVie (bass), Jeremy Spencer (guitar) and Peter Green (guitar). . . .

During 1969 Fleetwood Mac became a blues-rock band and began to gain a following outside of Europe. . . . [The] group signed to Warner Brothers and released *Then Play On,* their U.S. major-label debut, in September 1969. The following year frontman Peter Green left . . . Christine McVie . . . who recently married John McVie, came on as the band's keyboardist and backup vocalist. . . .

The revitalized Fleetwood Mac released the popular *Future Games* in the fall of 1971, quickly followed by 1972's *Bare Trees.* Now as big in America as in Europe, Fleetwood Mac began touring the U.S. . . . In 1975 the group brought in the soft rock duo Lindsey Buckingham (guitar) and Stevie Nicks (vocals), creating the band's classic lineup and shifting the band's sound towards pop. The new lineup made its debut on [the] 1975 album [*Fleetwood Mac*] which became their biggest hit to date, reaching No. 1 on the strength of the Top 20 singles "Rhiannon," "Over My Head," and "Say You Love Me" and eventually selling over five million copies.

Though both John and Christine McVie and Stevie and Lindsey Buckingham divorced, the band continued on, using their emotional turmoil as inspiration for their 1977 smash hit *Rumours.* The album spent 31 weeks at No. 1, selling over 17 million copies thanks to Top 10 singles "Go Your Own Way," "Don't Stop," "Dreams" and "You Make Loving Fun." Now at the 30 million sales mark, *Rumours* remains one of the top five best-selling albums of all time.

a genre known as classical rock, progressive rock, or art rock. And the style was enhanced by increasingly sophisticated recording equipment that allowed groups to overdub an ever-growing number of tracks.

Emerson, Lake, and Palmer (ELP), formed in 1970, was one of the first bands to wed rock and roll with the classical sounds of the nineteenth century. Classically trained keyboardist Keith Emerson pounded out cascades of intricate melodies that owed more to Beethoven than to Chuck Berry. Backed by the thundering drums of Carl Palmer and the sweet voice and melodic bass playing of Greg Lake, the group sold tens of millions of albums with such hits as "Lucky Man" and "The Three Fates."

Some of the symphony-length songs stretched out more than twenty minutes and were divided into three movements. And in concert, Emerson was a flamboyant showman who often stood between a piano and a Hammond B3 organ, playing both instruments simultaneously. At the fevered climax of a song, he might get behind the organ, play it upside-down, then rock the heavy instrument down onto his body and play it lying on the stage while Lake thrummed his bass furiously and Palmer's sticks exploded across the dozens of drums in his huge kit.

When ELP made a rocked-up album of *Pictures at an Exhibition,* a piece by nineteenth-century Russian composer Modest Mussorgsky, the marriage of rock and classical music was complete.

Saying Yes to Classical Rock

ELP was among several widely popular English classical rock groups during the early seventies. The group Jethro Tull, fronted by the flute-playing Ian Anderson, was huge in the United States, with albums such as *Benefit* in 1970, *Aqualung* in 1971, and *Thick as a Brick* in 1972. Like ELP, Jethro Tull backed up its advanced musical talents with hugely entertaining stage shows, led mostly by Anderson, as described by Tucker: "Onstage, Ian Anderson played the [extravagant] eccentric, letting his long, ratty hair sweep over his face as he huffed and puffed over his flute, glaring malevolently at the audience and abruptly whipping the flute behind his back to sing in a reedy, sarcastic tone."[38]

Although Anderson ridiculed religion and conformity and sang about homeless wastrels like "Aqualung," the rock group Yes purveyed a positive message of peace and love while wrapping its catchy songs in some of the most skillful playing to ever grace rock-and-roll albums. *The Yes Album,* released in 1971, was a masterpiece of musicianship. Songs such as "I've Seen All Good People" and "Yours Is No Disgrace" featured the sweet high vocals of Jon Anderson and the guitar work of Steve Howe, who wrung more notes from a guitar neck than anyone had previously thought possible. Bassist Chris Squire revolutionized the

The onstage antics of Jethro Tull's Ian Anderson, combined with the band's diverse musical talents, produced hugely entertaining stage shows.

concept of the instrument, playing rapid, melodic lines more like a lead guitarist.

By the mid to late seventies, however, most rock had collapsed under its own weight: The ostentatious excesses in the music simply overwhelmed many listeners. Although the genre faded quickly, songs such as "Lucky Man," "Aqualung," and "I've Seen All Good People" would continue to fill play lists on many AOR radio stations. By the late seventies the pretensions of the art rockers spawned the get-back-to-basics movement known as punk, played by people who believed rock and roll should be limited to three chords and a bad attitude.

The Singer-Songwriters

While rock got louder, heavier, and angrier during the seventies, the style known as singer-songwriter offered an antidote to those whose ears were ringing from screaming electric guitars.

The leader of the singer-songwriter movement was James Taylor, whose second album, *Sweet Baby James,* embraced all of the elements later made popular by the musical style. The album was low key, with bass and drums mixed way down behind the piano, acoustic guitar, and sweet, mellow vocals. The lyrics were personal and intimate, especially on the now-classic "Fire and Rain," a song Taylor wrote about a friend who died in an airplane crash.

Carol King was another leading singer-songwriter. King had made a name for herself as a songwriter for other groups, penning early sixties classics such as "Will You Love Me Tomorrow" and "Up on the Roof" with her then-husband Gerry Goffin. King became a superstar and a household name with the 1971 release of *Tapestry,* which contained the memorable songs "You've Got a Friend" and "(You Make Me Feel Like) A Natural Woman."

King became a role model for young women who wanted to break into the male-dominated recording industry. Many women were also inspired by Joni Mitchell, who started out as a folk rocker, singing about her own life and loves on albums such as 1970's *Ladies of the Canyon,* which was followed up by *Blue* the next year. Mitchell's song "Big Yellow Taxi," in which she sings about people paving paradise to put up a parking lot, was popular within the environmental movement, and her song "Woodstock," popularized by Crosby, Stills, Nash, and Young, became an anthem of a generation. Mitchell created a unique jazz-rock sound during the midseventies with albums such as *The Hissing of Summer Lawns, Hejira,* and *Don Juan's Reckless Daughter.* Although her innovative brand of music was misunderstood by some, Mitchell has influenced countless female artists, including Sarah McLachlan, Shawn Colvin, Sheryl Crow, k.d. lang, and others.

Dark Side of the Moon

While the art rock movement quietly faded away, one of its leading forces, Pink Floyd, went on to become the biggest band of all time. Pink Floyd had begun its musical career in 1966, playing psychedelic music in the college town of Cambridge, England, at "underground" parties where art students were dropping acid. After releasing the 1967 album *The Piper at the Gates of Dawn,* the band's recordings sold well in England but they were not well known in the United States. However, its follow-up albums, *A Saucerful of Secrets, Ummagumma, Atom Heart Mother,* and *Meddle,* sold moderately well in the United States, and the band toured college campuses and small auditoriums.

Pink Floyd's underground status quickly changed in 1973 with the release of its eighth album, *Dark Side of the Moon.* The album's theme was gloomy: The songs were about Pink Floyd founding member Syd Barrett's descent into mental illness. But the sonic pictures painted by the group on this album struck a chord with the masses. As Pink Floyd guitarist Dave Gilmore comments: "The words were brilliant, it had a lovely cover, and . . . [there] was something

Yes's music, a fusion of classical, jazz, and rock styles, combined a positive message of peace and love with some of the most skillful playing ever produced for a rock album.

Pink Floyd performs works from the album Dark Side of the Moon *in 1973. The album went on to become the longest selling album of all time, remaining on the charts for twelve hundred weeks.*

to appeal to everyone in the world in at least one of the songs, and everything gelled perfectly at that one moment."[39]

Pink Floyd toured relentlessly throughout the seventies, its stage shows growing in size and extravagance until the band constructed a huge wall onstage during performances of songs from the album *The Wall*. Although the band would break up in the early eighties, *Dark Side of the Moon* would go into the record books. It would remain on the *Billboard* charts for over twelve hundred weeks and continue to sell

nearly thirty years after its release, making it the longest-selling album of all time.

Heavy Metal Monsters of Rock

Whereas Pink Floyd was known for its onstage extravagance, heavy metal heroes Led Zeppelin was famous for its off-stage excesses, which often involved massive quantities of drugs and dozens of female fans known as groupies. Formed in Britain in 1969, Led Zeppelin took the heavy blues music of Howlin' Wolf and Willie Dixon and rewrote it for a new era. The group also fused the blues with folklore and Celtic mythology, producing FM radio staples such as "Stairway to Heaven."

Zeppelin flew along on the wings of Jimmy Page's fuzz-saturated staccato guitar riffs, John Paul Jones's bass barrage, John Bonham's arena-shattering drums, and Robert Plant's distorted, screaming vocals. Their blues-based heavy metal was worshiped by fans everywhere, and by the time the group released *Led Zeppelin III* in October 1970, it was the top rock act in the world.

Page was fascinated by the occult, and rumors spread that the band practiced black magic. When the instant success of Zeppelin spawned an army of heavy metal imitators, the occult became linked with the music style, especially with bands such as Black Sabbath. These early heavy metal bands spawned a massive group of imitators, such as Metallica, Megadeath, AC/DC,

The group Led Zepplin, with its blend of blues, celtic mythology folklore, and hard-driving rock and roll, spawned a new force in music, heavy metal.

Bruce Springsteen's Social Consciousness

Although MTV often emphasized glamour over substance, blue-collar rocker Bruce "the Boss" Springsteen reminded people that rock and roll had a responsibility to portray the concerns of everyday people. Springsteen synthesized the finest elements of fifties and sixties rock, combining the lonesome blues feel of fifties rocker Roy Orbison with the Wall of Sound production of Phil Spector and the discerning lyrics of Bob Dylan. And the singer was often referred to as "the next Dylan" during the 1970s, especially after his hit "Born to Run" was released in 1975.

The Boss was known for his high-energy stage shows, in which he appeared wearing simple blue jeans and T-shirts to prove that he did not need glitter rock to mesmerize an audience. Backed by the hard-rocking E Street Band, Springsteen's marathon shows often lasted three hours and featured the Boss jumping around the stage like an acrobat.

When Springsteen's videos, often live concert performances, appeared on MTV, they were a breath of fresh rock-and-roll air. With songs such as "Hungry Heart" and "Born in the U.S.A.," the Boss was one of the top-selling acts of the 1980s. But even as his songs topped the charts, Springsteen donated much of his time to raising funds for homeless Vietnam veterans, food shelves, the nuclear disarmament movement, Amnesty International, and various environmental causes. In an era of rock-and-roll excess, Springsteen reminded his fans that rock and roll could be about more than ostentatious living and accumulating wealth.

Bruce Springsteen is known for his high energy live performances and songs that portray the concerns of everyday people.

David Bowie performing as Ziggy Stardust in concert. Bowie almost single-handedly invented the genre known as glam rock.

and others. Each tried to outdo each other in outrageous behavior on and off stage.

Ziggy Plays Guitar

The excesses of bands like Led Zeppelin contributed to their reputation for testing boundaries, and band members' appearances enhanced that aura. Jimmy Page and Robert Plant pranced around the stage wearing tight pants, frilly shirts, and long curls, feminizing the image of rock stars. As the lines between male and female rock fashion began to blur during the early 1970s, David Bowie dropped into the middle of the scene portraying an androgynous space man on a mission.

Bowie, born David Jones in London in 1947, became an overnight sensation in 1972 with the release of *The Rise and Fall of Ziggy Stardust and the Spiders from Mars*. For the album, Bowie assumed the personality of a fictional character, Ziggy Stardust, who was supposed to be the biggest rock star in the world—and who just possibly was from outer space. In concert,

Bowie appeared in white face paint with his hair dyed carrot orange. He dressed in red knee-high platform boots and a brightly colored, skin-tight jump suit. In the process, Bowie became a rock star of unearthly proportions.

With this act, Bowie almost single-handedly invented the genre known as theatrical rock, glitter rock, or glam rock (for the glamorous fashion statements his clothing made). In this style of rock, the music was almost besides the point. Bowie commented on his invention in 1972: "My performances have got to be theatrical experiences for me as well as the audience. . . . I think it should be tarted up, made into a prostitute, a parody of itself. . . . I should be the clown. . . . The music is the mask the message wears . . . and I, the performer, am the message."[40]

Still, the album *Ziggy Stardust* was more than just theater. Bowie was a talented songwriter and an excellent singer with a unique vocal style.

By 1974 Bowie had abandoned his spaceman outfits in favor of stylish white suits. But once the glam rock genie was out of the bottle, it could not be contained. Singers such as Alice Cooper reveled in rock-and-roll theatrics. It was not unusual to see Cooper on stage in bizarre makeup, with a giant boa constrictor wrapped around his neck, or performing a mock execution of himself complete with a neck-chopping guillotine. The rock group Kiss took glam rock one step further, never appearing on stage without full face paint and outrageous costumes.

I Want My MTV

With the theatrical excesses of seventies rock stars creating a bigger sensation than the music they played, it was perhaps to be expected that television would become the venue of choice for many performers, especially as rapidly expanding cable service made far more program options available to viewers. With a relatively minor $20 million commitment from Warner Cable, a channel called MTV began showing videos that had been financed by artists as promotional items to sell records to twelve- to thirty-year-old consumers. When Music Television first went on the air on August 1, 1981, some in the industry doubted that people would want to "listen" to music on their televisions. They were quickly proven wrong, however. By 1983 MTV was seen in 17 million homes.

Although David Bowie was one of the early stars of MTV—his "Let's Dance" video was shown hourly in 1983—the music channel spawned a new generation of stars whose look and style received as much attention as the music. And the multitalented Michael Jackson proved to be perfectly suited to this new medium.

Jackson was a child prodigy who had recorded with his brothers in the hugely popular group Jackson 5 on the Motown label during the 1970s. Michael Jackson kept performing following the band's demise in 1976, and when Jackson recorded his solo

Prince Generates Controversy

Whereas Michael Jackson presented funk and soul music with a typical nonthreatening Motown formula, Prince shocked people in the conservative eighties with his outrageous brand of funk, punk, soul, and rock, fused together in an irresistible dance beat.

Prince Nelson was born in Minneapolis, Minnesota, in 1958, and by the time he was a teenager he was writing songs strongly influenced by the music of Jimi Hendrix and Sly Stone. Prince was also a wizard in the recording studio, writing, producing, and playing every instrument on a demo record he made when he was eighteen. After being signed by Warner Brothers, Prince released his first album, *For You,* in 1978, having played all twenty-seven instruments heard on the album himself.

Prince generated great controversy in 1979 with his third album, *Dirty Mind.* He appeared on the album cover wearing nothing but underwear and a raincoat, and the album's songs were full of sexually explicit lyrics. Radio programmers refused to play the album, but critics were smitten with the unique sound they dubbed "techno-funk."

The next year Prince hit the big time with the singles "1999," "Delirious," and "Little Red Corvette" from the double album *Controversy.* In 1984 the movie *Purple Rain* premiered. Prince had written and starred in the movie, and the album that accompanied the film sold 13 million copies in one year; the score also won an Oscar.

Prince remained incredibly popular throughout the eighties and nineties while releasing critically acclaimed albums. Although he generated controversy when he changed his name to an unpronounceable symbol in 1993, Prince's single-minded dedication to music has kept him among rock royalty since his first album.

album, *Off the Wall,* in 1979, his combination of musical styles such as soul, funk, and dance groove sold 6 million copies. In the process, the album became the biggest-selling record ever made by a solo African American artist.

Jackson's next album, *Thriller,* entered the *Billboard* top-ten chart on January 3, 1983, and stayed there for seventy-eight weeks—thirty-seven of those weeks at number one. Before the decade was over, *Thriller* had sold over 40 million copies and had become the best-selling record of all time. At one point it was selling 1 million copies a week. In March 1984 Jackson won a record eight Grammys for the album. Stephen Thomas Erlewine explains the reasons for *Thriller*'s huge success on the AMG All Music Guide website:

> This was a record that had something for everybody, building on the basic blueprint of *Off the Wall* by adding harder funk, hard rock, softer ballads, and smoother soul—expanding the approach to have something for every audience. That alone would have given the album a good shot at a huge audience, but it also arrived precisely when MTV was reaching its ascendancy, and Jackson helped the network by being not just its first superstar, but first black star. . . . This all would have made it a success (and its success, in turn, served as a new standard for success), but it

stayed on the charts, turning out singles, for nearly two years because it was really, really good.[41]

In videos shown on MTV, Jackson showed off his skillful dance moves on "Billie Jean," "Beat It," and "Thriller," and these set the standard for high-quality, well-produced videos for music television. As one critic commented at the time in the Canadian magazine *Maclean's,* "Videos have revived the demand for old fashion entertainment skills, an ideal situation for Jackson, who has been perfecting his act from the age of five."[42] By 1985 Jackson was one of the biggest rock stars the world had ever known, collecting armloads of Grammy and platinum record awards and a huge fortune along the way.

Madonna

Even parents approved of Jackson because of his conservative lifestyle: he neither drank, smoked, nor used drugs. However, a female artist performing at about the same time, Madonna, with her overt sexuality, outraged many parents when she first appeared on MTV. Like Jackson, Madonna created dance music with roots in funk and soul. She had a street smart sensibility and an inventive taste for fashion. With her arms dripping in bracelets and her funky secondhand-clothing-store fashions, Madonna's influence changed the way young women dressed virtually overnight.

After the success of her album *Like a Virgin* in 1984, Madonna appeared in the movie *Desperately Seeking Susan* and established herself as a movie star. Although her other movies, such as *Shanghai Surprise,* were flops, Madonna continued to generate songs that were number-one hits. She also remained a fixture on MTV. When she signed a $60-million record deal with

U2's Unforgettable Fire

The Irish band U2 defined rock's social consciousness during the eighties, and the group has remained at the top since that time, earning four Grammys in 2002 for "All That You Can't Leave Behind." Stephen Thomas Erlewine explains the band's success on the AMG All Music Guide website.

Through a combination of zealous righteousness and post-punk experimentalism, U2 became one of the most popular rock & roll bands of the '80s. Equally known for their sweeping sound as for their grandiose statement about politics and religion, U2 were rock & roll crusaders during an era of synthesized pop and heavy metal. [U2 guitarist] The Edge provided the group with a signature sound by creating sweeping sonic landscapes with his heavily processed, echoed guitars. . . . And their lead singer, Bono, was [a] frontman who had a knack of grand gestures that played better in arenas than small clubs. . .

. [There] rarely was a band that believed so deeply in the rock's potential for revolution as U2, and there rarely was a band that didn't care if they appeared foolish in the process. During the course of the early '80s, the group quickly built up a dedicated following through constant touring and a string of acclaimed records. By 1987, the band's following had grown large enough to propel them to the level of international superstars with the release of *The Joshua Tree.* Unlike many of their contemporaries, U2 was able to sustain their popularity in the '90s by reinventing themselves as a post-modern, self-consciously ironic dance-inflected pop-rock act, owing equally to the experimentalism of late '70s [David] Bowie and '90s electronic dance and techno. By performing such a successful reinvention, the band confirmed its status as one of the most popular bands in rock history, in addition to earning additional critical respect.

Time/Warner in 1992, Madonna became the highest-paid (at that time) pop diva in history.

With Madonna working for one of the largest companies in the world, the corporate control of rock was complete. From a counterculture musical festival performed in a farmer's field in Woodstock during the late sixties, rock and roll had grown into a multibillion-dollar industry in little more than two decades. What had started out as a revolution against the establishment had become mainstream, packaged, and sold. Although Madonna might raise eyebrows with her onstage persona, rock and roll was now as much a part of American culture as baseball—and it was seen by millions in the same stadiums where that popular sport is played.

Chapter Six

The Rise of Punk Rock

Rock and roll was almost completely consumed by commercial interests during the 1970s. Small record labels were bought up by huge media conglomerates, and as a result, only musical acts that could fill stadiums and sell millions of records received mainstream radio airplay. But many rock-and-roll musicians still harbored a strong rebellious streak, and some were not content to sit back and let corporate rock rule. Most of these individuals were alienated white kids in New York and London who saw a bleak future stretching out before them.

To some extent, the attitude of these young artists was a reflection of the times. The Vietnam War had ended in 1973, but returning veterans, along with other Americans, were confronted with high unemployment, inflation, and gasoline shortages. By the midseventies millions of workers had lost their jobs when steel mills and auto assembly lines shut down. At the same time, unemployment levels were soaring to their highest levels since the Great Depression during the 1930s, and skyrocketing interest rates were putting the dream of homeownership out of the reach of many. And when tax revenues dried up, big cities such as Cleveland, Detroit, and New York faced bankruptcy and were left without enough money to fix roads, repair schools, or place enough police on the streets to keep order.

The situation was worse in England, where power outages, strikes by garbage workers, and frighteningly high unemployment gripped the nation. For teenagers growing up during this decade, the sixties-era ideals of peace and love seemed like a joke. The anger and hopelessness that grew in place of that idealism fueled a new kind of music known as punk rock.

The Roots of Punk

Although punk rock gained momentum during the seventies, the founding members of the movement were in the

Velvet Underground, a band that was formed in 1965 by singer-songwriter Lou Reed, drummer Maureen Tucker, guitarist Sterling Morrison, and pianist/bassist/violist John Cale. As millions of Americans were dropping acid, growing long hair, and dressing like hippies, Reed tested the boundaries even more, writing songs about forbidden topics such as homosexuality, bisexuality, heroin addiction, transvestitism, and even death. His

The Velvet Underground, formed in 1965 and closely associated with artist Andy Warhol, wrote songs about previously forbidden subjects such as homosexuality, heroin addiction, and death.

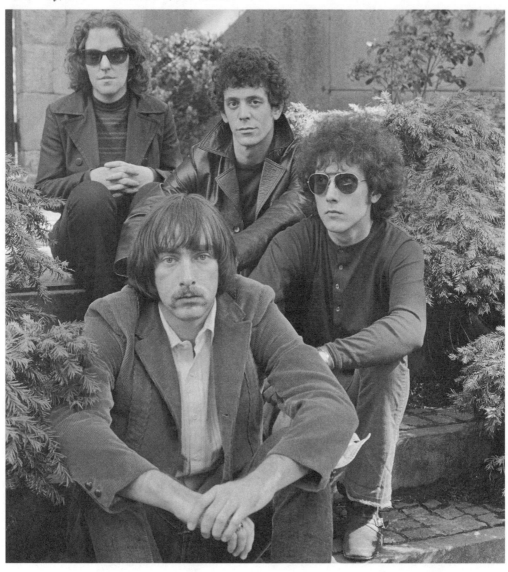

off-key, flat-toned, droll vocals were backed by an often sonic assault from the band that combined free-form jazz improvisation with two-chord rock, rhythm and blues, and avant-garde experimentation. In 1966 the group added a captivating German fashion model named Nico (who was also Reed's girlfriend) on vocals, and Reed penned some heart-rending love ballads for her to sing.

The Velvets were strongly influenced by the art movement known as minimalism, in which artists used basic colors and geometric shapes to produce uncluttered abstract paintings and sculptures. In music, this meant the use of simple rhythms and tones and repeated or sustained melodies that sometimes resulted in a hypnotic effect.

The Velvet Underground's minimalist sound attracted the renowned pop artist Andy Warhol when he heard the band playing at one of its early gigs in Greenwich Village. Warhol took over the band's management and used his considerable influence to book the Velvets at art gallery openings and underground movie screenings. Warhol also urged Reed to write songs about topics never before covered in song. As David Fricke writes in *The Rolling Stone Illustrated History of Rock,*

> [Warhol] encouraged Reed . . . to make the most of the opportunity to observe, and document, the circus of celebrities, star-struck socialites, sexual adventurers, dopers and art heads that congregated to Warhol's studio, the Factory.

Under Warhol's patronage, Reed had unlimited access to the underbelly of New York hip, in all its manic glory, and he made the most of it.[43]

When Warhol produced the group's 1967 debut album, *The Velvet Underground and Nico,* the cover simply featured a Warhol painting of a banana with a stick-on peel that could be pulled off. Unfortunately, the album was released at about the same time as the Beatles' groundbreaking *Sgt. Pepper's Lonely Hearts Club Band.* The Velvet Underground's album was largely overlooked as a result. Moreover, few people outside the New York artist underground were ready for the Velvet's combination of twisted love songs, white noise, and the celebration of sadomasochism and heroin.

After their first album, Nico left the Velvet Underground for a solo career, but the band's next album, *White Light/White Heat,* while selling very poorly at the time, would become one of the most influential proto-punk albums in history. While performing simple two- or three-chord songs, Reed spits, yells, and recites vocals in an almost raplike dirge while guitars wail and screech feedback in the mix. Raw, emotional, and musically unprofessional, this second and final album from the Velvet Underground would inspire nearly every punk rocker who followed in its wake. As Fricke writes,

Andy Warhol

The Andy Warhol Homepage contains the following information about the man who founded the pop art movement during the 1960s.

The American artist and film-maker Andy Warhol was born Andrew Warhola in 1928. . . . He is considered a founder and major figure of the POP ART movement. . . . In 1960 he produced the first of his paintings depicting enlarged comic strip images—such as Popeye and Superman—initially for use in a window display. Warhol pioneered the development of the process whereby an enlarged photographic image is transferred to a silk screen that is then placed on a canvas and inked from the back. It was this technique that enabled him to produce the series of mass-media images—repetitive, yet with slight variations—that he began in 1962. These, incorporating such items as Campbell's Soup cans, dollar bills, Coca-Cola bottles, and the faces of celebrities, can be taken as comments on the banality, harshness, and ambiguity of American culture.

Later in the 1960s, Warhol made a series of experimental films dealing with such ideas as time, boredom, and repetition; they include *Sleep* (1963), *Empire* (1964), and *The Chelsea Girls* (1966). In 1965 he started working with a rockband called "The Velvet Underground" formed by Lou Reed and John Cale. . . . Andy would travel around the country, not only with The Velvets, but also with superstar of the year Edie Sedgwick and the light-show "The Exploding Plastic Inevitable. . . . "

He founded *inter/VIEW* magazine in 1969 (they changed the name to *Interview* in 1971), published *The Philosophy of Andy Warhol: From A to B and Back Again* in 1975 and continued to paint portraits until his death in 1987.

There's a standing joke in rock & roll about the Velvet Underground:

Hardly anyone bought the group's records when they first came out, but the few people who did all went on to form their own bands. The real punchline is that just about every punk, post-punk and avant-pop artist or band of the past two decades [the eighties and seventies] owes a debt of inspiration, if not direct musical influence, to the Velvet Underground . . . arguably the most important American band . . . [and] the font from which nearly all white art beat noise of the Seventies and Eighties flows and the ruling standard for unfettered guitar ferocity and barbed narrative realism in rock songwriting.[44]

Detroit Kicks Out the Jams

While the Velvet Underground sang about the gritty side of New York City, a hard-rock, proto-punk anger was sweeping across the industrial Midwest. And that blind rage found its voice in the MC5.

Founded during the late 1960s, MC5 combined pounding heavy metal power chords, feedback, fuzzy grunge guitar, and a relentless rhythm section that could make listeners' ears ring. Based in Detroit, a tough, dirty city mired in crime, urban riots, and industrial decay, MC5 produced songs that preached the radical politics of anarchy and revolution. Their most famous song, "Kick Out the Jams," began with an obscenity that few middle-class record buyers used at that time. Although the band's music would become typical of MTV fare twenty or thirty years later, MC5 had little competition for Detroit's punk-rock crown in 1969.

The only artist who could be said to compete with MC5 was Iggy Pop, born James Newell Osterberg near Ann Arbor, Michigan, in 1947. Pop began his musical career as a blues drummer, but

he was always fascinated by odd noises, such as the sounds of a Detroit auto assembly line and even his father's electric razor. Inspired by Lou Reed's example, Pop decided to leave the drums behind and step out front as a lead singer. After founding the Psychedelic Stooges in 1967 (later shortened to the Stooges), Pop experimented making music on oil drums, vacuum cleaners, and other objects.

By this time Pop had discovered a way to attract attention to the Stooges' live act. While singing about isolation, discontentment, and sexual aggression over crunchy guitar rhythms, Pop slithered around on stage like a snake, pouring beer over his head, spitting it at the audience, and, sometimes, cutting his chest and arms with broken beer bottles. No one had ever seen an act like it, and fans urged Pop on to ever-more outrageous stunts, taunting him with screams and insults.

The Stooges were signed by Electra Records, and their self-titled debut album was produced by the Velvet Underground's John Cale. This album and the following one are mirror images of *White Light/White Heat*. Like the Velvets, however, the Stooges failed to make a mark on the record-buying public.

Pop soon left the Stooges, and after teaming up with David Bowie in 1972, Pop became an international celebrity. His music, along with that of the MC5 and the Velvet Underground, provided the sonic foundation for the punk movement that would follow.

Iggy Pop of the Stooges sang about isolation, discontentment, and sexual aggression while lacerating himself on stage.

CBGB—OMFUG

By the early seventies the center of the punk movement had moved back to New York City, specifically CBGB, a small club located on the run-down Bowery on Manhattan's Lower East Side. This neighborhood was full of abandoned buildings where winos, homeless drug ad-dicts, dealers, and hookers spent their days.

CBGB opened in 1973. Its full name, CBGB—OMFUG, was an acronym for music that was supposed to grace its stages—that is "Country, Bluegrass, Blues, and Other Music for Uplifting Gourmandizers." (A gorman-dizer is someone who eats greedily—a glutton—but in this case, it was meant to denote people who enthusiastically consumed music.)

Although few country or bluegrass bands ever played at the club, CBGB quickly attracted an underground rock scene made up of bands that played original music but lacked the connections that would allow them to play at more established Manhattan nightclubs, which only booked bands that had national label recording contracts. In contrast, the owner of CBGB only hired bands that played original music and had nowhere else to play.

The neighborhood surrounding CBGB had apartments with cheap rent, and struggling artists, actors, writers, poets, and musicians gravitated there. These people composed an instant fan base for the experimental bands that played at CBGB, such as Television, whose leader, Richard Hell, modeled the group's free jazz–style jams after the Velvet Underground. Hell also began the punk fashion aesthetic by wearing short, spiky hair and ripped up T-shirts held together with safety pins. Future Sex Pistol manager Malcolm McLaren describes Hell: "Here was a guy all deconstructed, torn down, looking like he just crawled out of a drain hole, looking like he was covered in slime, looking like he hadn't slept in years, looking like he hadn't washed in years."[45] Hell summed up his apathetic punk attitude with his song "(I Belong to) The Blank Generation," which became an anthem for those in the early punk movement.

Patti Smith's Punk Poetry

In addition to punk musicians' emphasis on attitude and appearances, there was an artistic element to their music that valued cleverness in the construction of lyrics. Patti Smith was one of the local poets who was attracted to the scene at CBGB. She had been reading her poetry in New York coffee houses since 1970, and in 1974 she inched toward rock and roll when she recited her poems backed by the guitar of Lenny Kaye on the single "Piss Factory." By 1975 Smith and Kaye had formed a band, and they were a regular attraction at CBGB. Smith's songs gained notice from Arista Records, and she was the first punk rocker to land a recording contract.

Smith's first album, *Horses,* produced by Cale, was released to wide critical acclaim. The album contains songs that feature her reedy voice singing and reciting her imaginative poetry over sparse musical arrangements. Smith also throws in a few punked-up rock classics such as "Land of a Thousand Dances," a sixties hit for soul artist Wilson Pickett, and "Gloria," by the Irish songster Van Morrison.

Smith's successive albums further cemented her reputation as a talented poet and musical innovator. In 1978 she teamed up with Bruce Springsteen to write "Because the Night," and this move catapulted her into the annals of rock stardom. Smith released the beautifully crafted *Dream of Life* in 1988, produced by her husband, MC5 founder Fred "Sonic" Smith.

Patti Smith performs at the CBGB Club in 1975. Her brand of poetry and unrestrained musical emotion would influence scores of punk musicians.

Throughout her long career, Patti Smith came to be considered a Dylanesque poet of punk, and her original brand of poetry and unbridled musical emotion would be emulated by scores of women and men during the years following her success.

The Ramones: Power Punk

Smith was the first punk artist to land a mainstream record contract, and the Ramones (a group of guys who all changed their last name to Ramone—Joey Ramone, Dee Dee Ramone, Marky Ramone, and so on) were the second. The Ramones played their first gig at CBGB in 1974, and they quickly became a featured act at the club. They dressed in tight jeans and black leather jackets with moptop Beatle hairdos. Although their look was hardly original, the Ramones stripped all pretension from rock music, their two-chord power pop sounding like psycho surfer music played by a demented Buddy Holly.

The Ramones played fast and loud, and with no one in the group competent enough to take solos, their sound consisted of a brick wall of earsplitting guitar chords hurled at the audience. Most of their songs clocked in at under two minutes, and their entire sets lasted less than twenty. Their sound was described in a review by James Wolcott in 1975, who wrote that the Ramones "play with a chopping [frenzy], the pace so brutal that the audience can barely catch its breath. A Ramones rampage is intoxicating—it's exciting to hear their voltage sizzle."[46]

The group had attracted enough attention by 1975 to secure a recording contract with Sire Records, and they made their first album, *The Ramones,* for less than six thousand dollars in early 1976. The mainstream American rock audience was not ready for the

Blondie

The following biography of the band Blondie was written by Fraser White and appears on the Blondie website.

Blondie was the most commercially successful band to emerge from the much vaunted punk/new wave movement of the late seventies. Along with bands such as Talking Heads, and the Sex Pistols, Blondie gets much of the credit for creating New Wave Punk, a late seventies, early eighties form of rock and roll that moved away from blues and extended guitar solos in favor of catchy tunes, thoughtful and humorous lyrics.

The prodigy of what was to become "Blondie" was founded in October 1973, when vocalist/songwriter, Deborah Harry . . . started both a musical and personal relationship with guitarist/songwriter Chris Stein. . . . They met after hanging around the punk birth place, the C.B.G.B. club. . . . [The] group "Blondie," was officially formed in New York City in August 1974. . . .

[In] 1976 [Blondie] released their brilliant self titled debut album. . . . [It] was seen as a vindication of "New Wave" punk rock, exploring (some would say exploiting) Debbie Harry's B-movie persona, and glamorous platinum blonde looks. The album was full of '60's influenced "girl group" tunes, fun, ironic all terms often used to describe this album. . . .

"Heart of Glass" from "Parallel Lines" their third album, was also their first world wide hit, going number one. . . . The disco song was seen not as a sell-out, but a send up, Blondie's keen sense of humour was still obvious. . . .

In 1979, Blondie's fourth album "Eat to the Beat" appeared accompanied by the first long-play video rock cassette of the whole album. . . . This superb album is pure raw energy, high adrenaline, in short pure rock, fun. . . .

In 1981 everyone took time off for their own projects. Debbie Harry recording her first solo record, "Koo Koo." [The group re-formed in 1999 to record the successful "No Exit."]

The Ramones played their music fast and loud at a frenzied pace.

now-classic punk anthems "Blitzkrieg Bop," "Beat on the Brat," "Judy Is a Punk," and "Chain Saw," and the album only reached number 111 on the *Billboard* charts.

When the Ramones toured Great Britain during the summer of 1976, however, disaffected English teenagers heard beauty in their music. When the band released its second album, *Ramones Leave Home,* in 1977, it barely registered in the United States, but it hit number forty-eight in England. With

catchy sing-along anthems such as "Pinhead," "Gimme Gimme Shock Treatment," and "Suzy Is a Headbanger," the Ramones planted the roots of punk in England that would create pandemonium on both sides of the Atlantic.

Johnny Rotten Hates Pink Floyd

During the summer of 1975, even before the Ramones had toured England, a British shopkeeper named Malcolm

The Talking Heads

The Talking Heads went from CBGB during the late seventies to major stardom on MTV during the 1980s. The following biography of the band appears on Rollingstone.com.

When David Byrne enrolled at the Rhode Island School of Design [RISD], he had no idea that this was the first step toward the future for the Talking Heads. It was there that he met Chris Frantz and Tina Weymouth with whom he would co-found the band.

The three left RISD for New York City in 1974 where they would get their big break opening up for the original punk band, The Ramones, at the infamous club CBGB's. Three years later, in 1977, the Talking Heads . . . released their first of many smash albums, *Talking Heads '77.* A year later, the band released *More Songs About Buildings and Food* their second album. Brian Eno produced *More Songs* and set it apart from what Talking Heads' contemporaries were doing by combining acoustic instruments with electronic ones and throwing in a tinge of funk.

It wasn't really until the early '80s that the Talking Heads would take the world by storm. The 1983 release of *Speakinq in Tongues* introduced one of the most popular songs ever written by the group, "Burning Down the House." Then in 1984, the band starred in and released the album for *Stop Making Sense,* a rockumentary about the group. Once again, catching the pop music wave, the band captivated American audiences with "Little Creature," which produced the fun-loving "And She Was," and the adoring "Stay Up Late," a song most likely about Byrne's newborn nephew.

A pioneer of music, Byrne experimented with many sounds during his stint with the Talking Heads. He added electronic instruments, funk, world music and heavy African percussion to their style. Over the course of their nearly 12-year career, the Talking Heads recorded 10 albums, releasing such great songs as "Psycho Killer." . . . In 1991, the Talking Heads officially announced their break up.

McLaren attended the CBGB rock festival, which featured forty bands that had no recording contracts. But McLaren was not there to hear the music. Instead, McLaren was looking for new and strange fashions to sell in his clothing store. He also tried to convince Richard Hell to move to England to front a band of McLaren's creation. When that failed, as British rock critic Pete Fame writes, "Hell refused—so McLaren borrowed his image."[47]

McLaren also saw an opportunity to make money off punk rock. Back in London, McLaren's shop—now named SEX and freshly stocked with punk fashions—began to attract artists; bored, angry teenagers; and rock-and-roll hopefuls. Among them were guitarist Steve Jones and drummer Paul Cook, who had been playing the music of Iggy Pop and the Stooges together since 1972. McLaren paired the two with bassist Glen Matlock, who worked behind the counter in the shop, and the band began looking for a lead singer who was shocking enough to gain the group some desperately needed publicity. McLaren seized on an angry, acne-faced store regular named John Lydon.

The green-haired nineteen-year-old, wearing a homemade shirt that bore the scrawled message "I Hate Pink Floyd," auditioned successfully by singing along with the Alice Cooper song "Schools Out." Because of the foul condition of his decaying teeth, Jones dubbed the singer Johnny Rotten. Meanwhile, McLaren stole the slogan of a T-shirt in the shop and named the band the Sex Pistols.

Adding Rotten to the band would prove to be a canny move. As Stephen Thomas Erlewine writes on the AMG All Music Guide,

> While the band played simple rock & roll loudly and abrasively, Rotten arrogantly sang of anarchy, abortion, violence, fascism, and apathy; without Rotten, the band wouldn't have been threatening to England's government—he provided the band's conceptual direction, calculated to be as confrontational and threatening as possible.[48]

Above all, Rotten personified the punk image. Onstage he taunted the audience, screamed insults, spit beer, and threw himself about on the stage, bouncing off amps and drums like a rag doll. The Pistols dressed in the most punkish outfits they could fashion, with marching boots reminiscent of those worn by Nazi stormtroopers, shredded jeans, and studded leather jackets smeared with obscene graffiti.

Anarchy in the United Kingdom

The group was signed by EMI in 1976 and received a forty-thousand-dollar advance before releasing its first single, "Anarchy in the UK." In the song, Rotten screams that he is an anarchist and the anti-Christ. When the members of the Sex Pistols appeared extremely drunk on an early evening live television talk show to promote the song, they unloaded a stream of foul language that shocked the audience. This story made front-page headlines the next day, and EMI dropped the band immediately. The bad publicity caused promoters across the United Kingdom to drop the group from its planned "Anarchy National Tour."

In the interim, the group decided that bassist Matlock was far too clean-cut for the band's raunchy image. He was fired and replaced by Sid Vicious who, although he was unable to play bass, was the perfect foil for Rotten. Vicious lived up to his name, gouging himself

with beer bottles and cracking heads in the audience with his heavy Fender bass guitar.

In March 1977 the band released "God Save the Queen." This song, which savaged the revered queen of England, created even more controversy in a nation where insulting the queen was tantamount to burning the flag. Worse, the record sleeve depicted the queen's face with a safety pin through her nose. Although the song was banned by British radio stations, it soared to number one in sales. The Sex Pistols' insulting portrayal of the queen made Rotten and Vicious the targets of

The Sex Pistols' raw and violent performances changed the landscape of rock and roll and gave birth to a new musical underground.

physical violence, and they were beaten and cut during assaults by total strangers wielding pipes and razors.

The band released *Never Mind the Bollocks—Here's the Sex Pistols* in 1977 and played a tour of the United States in 1978. By this time Vicious was a heroin addict; he was often so high that he was barely able to stand up onstage. Rotten, sick of the controversy that followed the band, quit after the group's last gig in San Francisco.

The Sex Pistols lasted little over two years, but as Erlewine writes,

[They] changed the face of popular music. Through their raw, nihilistic singles and violent performances, the band revolutionized the idea of what rock & roll could be. . . . [Countless] bands in [England and America] were inspired by the sheer sonic force of their music. . . . The band gave birth to the massive independent music underground in England and America that would soon include bands that didn't have a direct mu-

sical connection to the Sex Pistols' initial three-minute blasts of rage, but couldn't have existed without those singles.[49]

After the breakup of the band, Vicious died of a heroin overdose in February 1979, and Rotten went on to form the band Public Image Limited. An excellent documentary of the band's rise and fall, *The Filth and the Fury,* was released in 2000.

The Sex Pistols exhibited the ultimate expression of the punk attitude that embraced raw emotion, unflinching social commentary, and basic three-chord rock and roll. Artists like the Ramones, Patti Smith, the Talking Heads, and others rescued rock and roll from 1970s pretentiousness and went on to influence hundreds of bands in later decades, including Nirvana and Green Day. The style that began with Lou Reed in the New York artist underground during the 1960s went on to make headlines across the globe. In the meantime, it spawned a movement that changed the world of music.

Chapter Seven

Rock's Next Generation

Although the youngsters known as the baby boom generation dominated rock and roll from the 1950s through the 1980s, by 1990 these boomers were in their thirties and forties, hardly an age group that might be expected to create groundbreaking music. The children of the boomers, dubbed Generation X by social commentators, were coming of age, and their perspectives and expectations were totally different from those of the post–World War II generation. The children of the baby boomers grew up in an era of high divorce rates, AIDS, gang violence, and destructive drugs such as crack. In addition, three severe recessions in the United States during the eighties and early nineties created unemployment that left many young people with diminished economic prospects. The music of this era, such as hard-core punk, metal, grunge, and rap, reflected the anger of the X Generation. As founder of Sub Pop Records Jonathan

Poneman stated in 1992, "[When you] see a lot of [your] dreams subside because of this particularly brutal recession, and class warfare, race warfare, it makes you very angry, very fearful, very alienated. And those are qualities that lead to an unusually rebellious passionate rock."[50]

Hard-Core Punk

During the 1980s, when political leaders in America were promoting a return to old-fashioned "family" values, nothing was more defiant than hard-core punk. While record companies promoted the "safe," middle-of-the-road sounds of Huey Lewis and the News, Hall and Oates, and Billy Joel, a burgeoning hard-core scene was fermenting in many American cities. And some of these bands made the Sex Pistols seem almost tame by comparison.

Lyrics to hard-core punk songs were aimed at the angry, desperate, and alienated among America's youth. The music was played as loudly as possible and accompanied by whatever stage antics generated the most shock. Hardcore performers might appear onstage wielding chainsaws and dressed in vinyl, plastic, black leather—or nothing at all. Following in the footsteps of Johnny Rotten and Syd Vicious, hardcore musicians adopted names such as Don Bonebreak, Darby Crash, and Pat Smear. And the names of the bands, such as X, Germ, Bad Religion, and Black Flag (named after a popular household insecticide), spoke volumes about the music they performed. Song titles, too, reflected the attitude of the music. For example, Black Flag performed songs with searing titles such as "Depression," "Revenge," "Dead Inside," and "Life of Pain." Henry Rollins, who wrote these songs, describes his motivation:

[I'm] a classic product of a typical dysfunctional family. I don't know jack . . . about love, or about feeling a relationship with a blood relative. That . . . means nothing to me. . . .

Pain is my girlfriend; that's how I see it. . . . I feel pain every day of my life. When you see me perform, it's that pain you're seeing coming out. I put all my emotions, all my feelings, and my body on the line. People hurt me. I hurt myself—mentally, physically.[51]

Since record companies refused to touch bands like Black Flag, hard-core groups started their own independent record labels to distribute their music. Some, as it turned out, were quite successful. For instance, Bad Religion started Epitaph Records, which sold 7 million copies of the band's album *Smash*.

The hard-core scene, which started in Los Angeles, soon spread to other cities throughout the United States. In Minneapolis, bands such as Husker Du and the Replacements melded heavy metal power chords with punk and hard-core. In San Francisco the Dead Kennedys, led by singer Jello Biafra, mixed hard-core music with ironic left-wing social commentary in songs such as "Kill the Poor," "Lynch the Landlord," and "Terminal Preppie."

The attitude of hard-core punk was that anybody could play the music, and the walls between audience and performer were broken down. This led to a new form of violent physical expression seen in front of stages when hard-core bands performed. As Biafra states, "[When] younger people [started] coming to our shows in droves, they brought the arena rock mentality with them, including fights [and] jumping off the stage just to see if you could hit people."[52] This led to audience members slamming into each other, or "moshing."

The Heaviest Metal
Meanwhile, in England the hard-core attitude was expressed by various bands that played a harder version of heavy metal. Known as thrash metal

Spinal Tap Mocks Heavy Metal

In 1984 comedians Michael McKean, Christopher Guest, and Harry Shearer wrote and starred in *Spinal Tap*, a movie that mercilessly ridiculed the British heavy metal rock scene of the early eighties. Dubbed a "mockumentary" because it was a mock documentary, the movie portrayed the comeback American tour of the fictional has-been band Spinal Tap. With silly long-hair wigs and pasted-on facial hair, Spinal Tap played ridiculous song parodies, such as "Smell the Glove," "Gimme Some Money," "Big Bottom," and "Sex Farm," from their album *This Is Spinal Tap*. Their drummers tended to burst into flames, and they remained clueless as to their extremely politically incorrect behavior.

With the success of their movie, the band continued with the joke for decades, releasing the album *Break Like the Wind* in 1992 and playing concerts on the "Back from the Dead" tour in 2000. And like all great rock bands, real or imagined, Spinal Tap was featured on an episode of the television show *The Simpsons* in 1992.

or, in England, the New Wave of British Heavy Metal, this music was loud and theatrical. The blues-based music relied on lead singers who could shriek high-pitched vocals over fuzz-tone power chords and a pounding rhythm section. Like hard-core punkers, thrash metal musicians were generally from the poorer classes and were well acquainted with unemployment, domestic violence, and social alienation. As was true of punk rock, there was no wall between the fans and the musician. People at thrash metal concerts pumped their fists in the air, moshed, and jumped headlong from the stage, hoping the crowd would catch them.

With little support from record companies, thrash metal was an underground movement whose fans kept informed through cheap paper magazines called fanzines. In an age before the World Wide Web, these fanzines allowed thrash metal fans to find out about upcoming concerts, their favorite bands, thrash fashion, and other news.

Thrash metal took off in London during the early 1980s with bands such as Judas Priest, Iron Maiden, and Motorhead. Around the same time, Australian metal rockers AC/DC hit the British top ten with the album *Highway to Hell.* AC/DC continued its success in the United States, hitting the U.S. top ten with its next albums, *Back in Black* and *For Those About to Rock (We Salute You).*

Thrash Metal Speeds Up

By the mid-1980s Los Angeles–based Metallica had added a new twist to thrash metal, playing as fast as possible in a style dubbed "speed metal," "black metal," or even "grindcore," depending on the fanzine that was covering the band. Metallica released *Kill 'em All* in 1983, and by 1988 the band, which received no radio play or MTV exposure, hit the top ten by selling 9 million copies of *And Justice for All.* The success of Metallica opened doors for dozens of other thrash metal bands, including Anthrax, Def Leppard, Megadeth, Poison, Ratt, and Slaughter.

By the end of the eighties, metal had entered the mainstream of rock and roll as the Guns n' Roses (GNR) video of "Sweet Child o' Mine" received heavy rotation on MTV, pushing sales of the album *Appetite for Destruction* into the stratosphere. Although the music was toned down from the "death metal" of bands like Metallica, GNR singer Axl Rose created controversy with his sexist, homophobic, and bigoted lyrics.

As metal became more popular, conservative social critics assailed the music for its lyrics, which some claimed drove teens to irresponsible sex, drug use, and even suicide. Although no research backed up these accusations, thrash metal bands remained a thorn in the side of parents and authority figures throughout the eighties and nineties, while selling millions of records to teens who delighted in shocking adults with this harsh new sound.

Grunge and Alternative

Thrash metal was as politically incorrect as possible and was meant to generate controversy. Meanwhile, a more thoughtful hybrid of hard-core punk and metal, known as grunge, or alternative rock, came bursting out of Seattle during the early 1990s. And record sales by alternative bands would easily equal those of the thrashers.

Grunge, so named because of its sludgy, fuzzy sound, got its start at the independent record label Sub Pop, named after a fanzine *Subterranean Pop,* first published by Bruce Pavitt in Olympia, Washington, during the early 1980s. In 1986 Pavitt joined with Jonathan Poneman to launch Sub Pop Records in order to distribute cassettes and short vinyl albums, known as EPs (extended plays), made by local musicians.

Sub Pop first made waves in 1987 with the grunge group Soundgarden, whose hybrid sound was described by Stephen Thomas Erlewine on the (AMG) All Music Guide website:

[Soundgarden] developed directly out of the grandiose blues-rock of Led Zeppelin and the sludgy, slow riffs of Black Sabbath. Which isn't to say they were a straightahead metal band. Soundgarden borrowed the . . . aesthetics of punk, melding their guitar-driven sound with an intelligence and ironic sense of humor. . . . Furthermore, the band rarely limited themselves to simple, pounding riffs, often making detours into psychedelia. But the group's key sonic signatures—the gutsy wail of vocalist Chris Cornell and the winding riffs of guitarist Kim Thayil—were what brought the band out of the underground.[53]

After recording several popular underground EPs for Sub Pop, Soundgarden was signed by a major label, and although its debut album, *Louder than Love,* only reached 108 on the charts, it received a Grammy nomination in 1989.

Nirvana's brand of grunge rock made them one of the favorites of MTV's audience.

Although critics expected Soundgarden to take alternative rock into the mainstream, the band was eclipsed by the unexpected success of Nirvana's *Nevermind* in 1991. The album, which eventually sold more than 7 million copies in the United States alone, was pushed to the top of the charts by the catchy "Smells Like Teen Spirit," the first anthem of grunge. Propelled forward by a memorable video of the song, Nirvana became the darling of MTV, and in 1992 the group was the first grunge band to make it onto the cover of *Rolling Stone* magazine. Nirvana's emotional sound, driven by the songs of lead singer Kurt Cobain, was at times raucous and intense, angst-ridden and bleak. Cobain, a heroin addict, projected a vulnerable yet volatile image.

Nirvana's main competition came from another Seattle-area band, Pearl Jam, whose 1992 album, *Ten,* sold 9 million copies, propelled by the rich, soaring vocals of lead singer Eddie Vedder. In 1993 Pearl Jam broke first-week sales records as its second album, *Vs.,* entered the national charts at number one, selling more than 950,000 copies within seven days of its release.

With alternative rock topping the charts, grunge clothing, such as heavy boots called Doc Martens, ripped flannel shirts, torn jeans, knit caps, mismatched stripes, and unkempt hair, made it into a *Vogue* magazine fashion spread. Several big-name New York fashion designers adopted the look for their fashion shows.

The darker side of grunge came to the public's consciousness, however, when Cobain's stress from sudden stardom, his relationship with his wife, Courtney Love, and his heroin addiction pushed him into a deep depression. Despite the publicity his problems received, grunge fans were stunned on April 8, 1994, when Cobain was found dead from a self-inflicted gunshot wound.

Cobain's death did not prevent grunge's gradual move into the mainstream of rock and roll. But Pearl Jam, who had become the main focus of the grunge movement, took steps to lower its profile. The band began to tour only sporadically, refused to make rock videos, and generally shunned media attention.

The Women of Lilith Fair

Grunge challenged many of the values of mainstream culture, but as had been the case through much of the rock-and-roll era, its biggest stars were mostly men. In fact, women had always struggled in the male-dominated world of rock and roll. For years, radio and record executives had believed that there was limited demand for female artists, and they maintained informal quotas as a result. Although they would sign dozens of male bands, most record labels would only sign one female rocker per year. And radio stations limited the number of female artists on their playlists—for example, almost never playing records by two women back to back. Yet a new generation of female artists who came into their own during the 1990s proved that female artists could compete successfully with macho rock stars when given a chance.

Whereas some women, such as Madonna, used sex to sell music, Canadian singer Sarah McLachlan relied on well-crafted songs that were closer to folk rock than grunge. Her 1988 album, *Touch,* achieved a gold record in Canada, and her 1993 effort, *Fumbling Towards Ecstasy,* spent sixty-two weeks on the charts and reached platinum status both in Canada and the United States.

McLachlan, however, was frustrated that she could not get her music played on male-dominated radio stations. And she was fed up with the concert industry, which refused to put more than one female artist on a tour, only using women to warm up for male-dominated bands. In 1997 McLachlan defied conventional wisdom, which held that an all-female roster would not sell tickets, and began producing the Lilith Fair, a rock festival whose featured acts were all women.

Lilith Fair, named after Adam's first wife of Hebrew legend, grossed $16 million in thirty-eight shows, nearly

Lollapalooza

The success of alternative rock generated alternative rock festivals during the 1990s. The first such festival was the multicultural Lollapalooza, which combined rap, punk medal, and a wide variety of other musical styles. Lollapalooza was first established during the summer of 1991 by Jane's Addiction singer Perry Farrell. No one thought that seven bands from seven clashing musical styles could prove successful—even if they did share alternative roots. But the festival worked, and it effected a change in pop music.

The premier Lollapalooza tour was headlined by Ice-T's Body Count, English goth-rockers Siouxsie and the Banshees, black jazz-metal fusion players Living Colour, punk-metal guitarist Henry Rollins, and scene-stealers Nine Inch Nails. The shows went smoothly, there were few culture clashes, and fans loved their newfound multicultural power. But by 1998 Farrell called it quits, announcing he could not find enough talent for another Lollapalooza.

Frustration with the refusal of male dominated radio stations to play her songs led Sarah McLachlan to produce Lilith Fair in 1997.

nie Raitt, and Emmylou Harris. The 1998 Lilith Fair covered fifty-seven U.S. shows. It later tested markets in Japan, Australia, and Europe.

Concert promoters were reluctant to book the Lilith Fair. They thought it would be unsuccessful. Singer Shawn Colvin states, "We always knew that it wasn't true . . . that it was just sexist to think you couldn't have women on the same bill. It was just a matter of time before it would be proven false, and I'm only glad I was around when it happened. It's like an albatross being taken off your neck."[54]

Lilith's success was helped by the fact that women had become the largest purchasers of CDs, growing from 43 percent in 1988 to 51.4 percent in 1998. At the same time, many believed that women were producing some of the freshest music heard in years. The Lilith Fair—which attracted 70 percent women, mostly ages seventeen to thirty-five—brought women back into the mainstream of music and gave voice to great talents that until that time had been too often ignored by the music industry.

doubling the take of the male-dominated alternative music festival Lollapalooza. A two-disc CD, featuring live performances from Lilith, grossed another $4 million. Lilith featured a who's who of award-winning female rockers, including Jewel, Paula Cole, Shawn Colvin, Heather Nova, the Indigo Girls, Fiona Apple, Sheryl Crow, Suzanne Vega, Tracy Chapman, Bon-

Rap and Hip Hop

Just as the large corporations that dominated the rock-music business had discriminated against women, inner-city blacks had also been long ignored by the major labels during the eighties and nineties. Although mainstream acts like Michael Jackson were popular, few record companies were interested in the hip-hop culture and rap music that had evolved in New York's depressed Bronx district during the late seventies.

Rap music's roots run the deepest of all forms of rock and roll since it is based on the traditions of ancient African storytellers known as griots, who were able to poetically recite tribal histories and the great deeds of warriors and kings. This tradition has long run through African American music and has evolved in the modern world into rap, described by Tricia Rose in *Black Noise:*

> Rap music brings together a tangle of some of the most complex social, cultural, and political issues in contemporary American society. . . . Rap music is a black cultural expression that prioritizes black voices from the margins of urban America. Rap music is a form of rhymed storytelling accompanied by highly rhythmic, electronically based music. It began in the mid-1970s in the South Bronx in New York City as a part of hip hop, an African-American and Afro-Caribbean youth culture composed of graffiti, breakdancing, and rap music.[55]

During the 1990s rap's first successful mainstream album was *The Chronic* by Dr. Dre, a former producer-rapper from the group called NWA. Dre produced the album on his own Death Row record label, and the album went mulitplatinum. Dre used the album as a springboard to promote other Death Row artists, including Snoop Doggy Dogg and the Dogg Pound.

The label, owned by Time Warner, was later to find itself at the center of the 1995 media firestorm over responsibility for crimes inspired by violent lyrics of Death Row artists. Rose explains the motivation for the controversial subject matter and lyrics:

> From the outset, rap music has articulated the pleasures and problems of black urban life in contemporary America. Rappers speak with the voice of personal experience, taking on the identity of the observer or narrator. Male rappers often speak from the perspective of a young man who wants social status in a locally meaningful way. They rap about how to avoid gang pressures and still earn local respect, how to deal with the loss of several friends to gun fights and drug overdoses, and they tell grandiose and sometimes violent tales that are powered by male sexual power over women.[56]

Growing up in this urban environment affected many rappers even after they achieved fame and fortune, including Tupac Shakur, one of rap's biggest stars. Shakur, under the name 2Pac, recorded his first gold record, *2Pacalypse Now,* in 1991. The U.S. vice president at the time, Dan Quayle, publicly claimed that the album's inflammatory lyrics about shooting police officers had influenced the killer of a Texas policeman.

Shakur's violent "thug" life plagued his successful recording career. He was arrested several times, shot four times during a Manhattan robbery, and was finally gunned down on September 7, 1996, in Las Vegas.

Despite the agitation it caused many social critics, rap continued to work its way into mainstream American consciousness, and groups like Wu-Tang Clan sold millions of records during the 1990s. By the end of the nineties, rap music by the Notorious BIG, Wyclef Jean, Scarface, and other rappers made up 10 to 15 percent of all CD sales. Female rappers also got into the game with Queen Latifah, Sister Souljah, Little Kim, and Foxy Brown achieving major success.

Dr. Dre, former producer/rapper with the group NWA, started Death Row records and brought rap into the mainstream of popular music.

Like other forms of music since the 1980s, rap generated several related genres by fusing with other styles to form hybrids such as the electronically generated sounds of techno hop and psychedelic trip hop (rap music over electronic techno music).

Rock's Fourth Generation

During the early years of the twenty-first century, rock and roll is more diverse than ever and the boundaries between musical styles have all but vanished. Beck utilizes a hybrid style of rap, blues, rock, and even country on his albums, such as *Odelay* and *Midnight Vultures*. Teen sensations like NSync pepper their soulful sixties-style harmonies with hip-hop rhythms. Meanwhile, rap group Public Enemy uses samples from songs by the thrash metal band Anthrax as a backdrop for its hard-core urban poetry. No Doubt, led by the irrepressible Gwen Stefani, combines the danceable beat of Jamaican ska music with good old rock and roll.

Rock music today has morphed into almost anything its fans want it to be. Instead of single artists, such as Elvis or the Beatles, dominating the *Billboard* charts, fans can find music of obscure bands on the Internet and follow their careers online. Meanwhile, musicians

Public Enemy

Public Enemy produced some of the most powerful rap music of the eighties and nineties. The following biography of the band was published on Rollingstone.com.

Often considered one of the most controversial and influential groups in rap music, Public Enemy started the trend that blurred the lines between music and politics, channeling hip-hop as a social force.

As a graphic arts student in New York, Chuck D . . . met fellow hip-hop fans Hank Shocklee and Bill Stepheny while deejaying at a college radio station. The three cut several demos, catching the eye of producer Rick Rubin. Impressed by Chuck D's freestyling, he recruited the rapper to his up-and-coming Def Jam label. While Shocklee and Stepheny signed on as producer and publicist, respectively, Chuck D recruited DJ Terminator X . . . Professor Griff . . . and Flavor Flav . . . to round out the crew.

While the group was officially formed in 1982, they didn't cut an album until 1987's Yo! Bum Rush the Show. Though it met with critical praise, the album failed commercially on all charts. However, their 1988 follow-up, It Takes Millions to Hold Us Back was considered revolutionary. With production team the Bomb Squad, Public Enemy found a sound that mixed off-beat samples and classic funk, while playing up the interaction between Chuck D's political rhetoric and Flavor Flav's off-the-wall humor. . . .

Public Enemy's 1990 album Fear of a Black Planet generated enthusiastic response, hitting the pop Top 10. 1991's Apocalypse 91 . . . The Enemy Strikes Black, continued the crossover success with a remade version of "Bring the Noize" featuring the metal band Anthrax. . . .

[In] 1994, Chuck D retired the group from touring, broke away from Def Jam to start his own label and released his solo debut The Autobiography of Mista Chuck.

Public Enemy, shown in concert, produced some of the most powerful rap in the eighties and nineties–and the most controversy.

no longer need record companies to be heard. They can produce music cheaply and efficiently on their home computers, burn CDs for distribution, or post the music on a file-swapping website.

Fifty years after Bill Haley sang "Rock Around the Clock," rock and roll has become an integral part of the world culture and has extended its reach to every corner of the globe. And to paraphrase the lines of the "Killer," Jerry Lee Lewis, more than ever there is a whole lotta shakin' goin' on!

• Notes •

Chapter One: The Roots of Rock

1. Hoy Hoy, "Wynonie Harris" www.hoyhoy.com.
2. James Miller, *Flowers in the Dustbin: The Rise of Rock and Roll, 1947–1977.* New York: Simon and Schuster, 1999, p. 92.
3. Quoted in Robert K. Oermann, *A Century of Country.* New York: TV Books, 1999, p. 136.
4. Quoted in William McKeen, ed., *Rock and Roll Is Here to Stay.* New York: W.W. Norton, 2000, p. 29.
5. Quoted in Oermann, *A Century of Country,* p. 142.
6. Quoted in Linda Martin and Kerry Segrave, *Anti-Rock.* Hamden, CT: Archon Books, 1988, p. 76.
7. Quoted in David P. Szatmary, *Rockin' in Time: A Social History of Rock and Roll.* New York: Schirmer Books, 2000, p. 18.
8. Quoted in Martin and Segrave, *Anti-Rock,* p. 73.
9. Quoted in Mark Jacobson, "Chuck Berry, the Father of Rock Turns Seventy-Five," *Rolling Stone,* December 6, 2001, p. 80.

Chapter Two: The Beatles and the British Invasion

10. Quoted in Martin and Segrave, *Anti-Rock,* p. 44.

11. Quoted in The Beatles, *The Beatles Anthology.* San Francisco: Chronicle Books, 2000, p. 11.
12. Quoted in The Beatles, *The Beatles Anthology,* p. 49.
13. Quoted in Pete Shotten and Nicholas Schaffner, *John Lennon in My Life.* New York: Stein and Day, 1983, p. 69.
14. Shotten and Schaffner, *John Lennon in My Life,* p. 68.
15. George Martin, *With a Little Help from My Friends: The Making of Sgt. Pepper.* New York: Little, Brown, 1994, p. 157.
16. Quoted in Szatmary, *Rockin' in Time,* p. 111.

Chapter Three: Sweet Sixties Soul

17. Quoted in Gerri Hirshey, *Nowhere to Run.* New York: Times Books, 1984, p. 49.
18. Quoted in Anthony DeCurtis and James Henke with Holly George-Warren, eds., *The Rolling Stone Illustrated History of Rock.* New York: Random House, 1992, p. 131.
19. Quoted in DeCurtis and Henke, *The Rolling Stone Illustrated History of Rock,* p. 132.
20. Quoted in Hirshey, *Nowhere to Run,* p. 50.

21. Quoted in Hirshey, *Nowhere to Run,* p. 47.
22. Quoted in DeCurtis and Henke, *The Rolling Stone Illustrated History of Rock,* p. 281.
23. Quoted in Szatmary, *Rockin' in Time,* pp. 130–31.

Chapter Four: Folk Rock Turns Psychedelic

24. Michael Gray, *Song and Dance Man III.* London: Cassell, 2000, p. 17.
25. Gray, *Song and Dance Man III,* p. 4.
26. Gray, *Song and Dance Man III,* p. 4.
27. Quoted in DeCurtis and Henke, *The Rolling Stone Illustrated History of Rock,* p. 300.
28. Quoted in David Bauder, "New Game Is Blowin' on the Web," *Los Angeles Times,* February 22, 2002, p. F14.
29. Quoted in DeCurtis and Henke, *The Rolling Stone Illustrated History of Rock,* p. 309.
30. Quoted in Jim DeRogatis, *Kaleidoscope Eyes.* New York: Citadel, 1996, p. 48.
31. Quoted in DeCurtis and Henke, *The Rolling Stone Illustrated History of Rock,* p. 316.
32. Quoted in Jann Wenner, ed., *20 Years of Rolling Stone: What a Long, Strange Trip It's Been.* New York: Straight Arrow, 1987, p. 37
33. Quoted in Szatmary, *Rockin' in Time,* p. 153.

34. Quoted in DeRogatis, *Kaleidoscope Eyes,* p. 54.
35. Quoted in DeRogatis, *Kaleidoscope Eyes,* p. 57.

Chapter Five: Rock-and-Roll Superstars

36. Ed Ward, Geoffrey Stokes, and Ken Tucker, *Rock of Ages: The Rolling Stone History of Rock.* New York: Rolling Stone, 1986, p. 486.
37. Ward, Stokes, and Tucker, *Rock of Ages,* p. 469.
38. Ward, Stokes, and Tucker, *Rock of Ages,* p. 481.
39. Quoted in DeRogatis, *Kaleidoscope Eyes,* p. 72.
40. Quoted in Miller, *Flowers in the Dustbin,* p. 299.
41. Stephen Thomas Erlewine, "Thriller," AMG All Music Guide. www.allmusic.com.
42. Quoted in Szatmary, *Rockin' in Time,* p. 251.

Chapter Six: The Rise of Punk Rock

43. Quoted in DeCurtis and Henke, *The Rolling Stone Illustrated History of Rock,* p. 352.
44. Quoted in DeCurtis and Henke, *The Rolling Stone Illustrated History of Rock,* p. 348.
45. Quoted in Szatmary, *Rockin' in Time,* p. 226.
46. Quoted in Tricia Henry, *Break All the Rules: Punk Rock and the Making of a Style.* Ann Arbor, MI: UMI Research Press, 1989, p. 57.

47. Quoted in Henry, *Break All the Rules,* p. 59.
48. Stephen Thomas Erlewine, "The Sex Pistols," AMG All Music Guide. www.allmusic.com.
49. Erlewine, "The Sex Pistols."

Chapter Seven: Rock's Next Generation
50. Quoted in Szatmary, *Rockin' in Time,* p. 274.
51. Quoted in Szatmary, *Rockin' in Time,* pp. 274–75.
52. Quoted in Szatmary, *Rockin' in Time,* pp. 277.
53. Stephen Thomas Erlewine, "Soundgarden," AMG All Music Guide. www.allmusic.com.
54. Quoted in Robert Hillburn, "They Said She Couldn't Do It," *Los Angeles Times,* June 21, 1998, Sunday Calender section, p. 4.
55 Tricia Rose, *Black Noise.* Hanover, NH: Wesleyan University Press, 1994, p. 2.
56. Rose, *Black Noise,* p. 2.

• For Further Reading •

The Beatles, *The Beatles Anthology.* San Francisco: Chronicle Books, 2000. This book offers four hundred large pages of rare photos and insightful text by the Beatles about the Beatles. As the book's dust-cover says, "The Beatles' story told for the first time in their own words and pictures."

Richard Carlin, *Rock and Roll, 1955–1970.* New York: Facts On File, 1988. The history of rock and roll during the exciting and innovative early decades.

Nicole Claro, *Madonna.* New York: Chelsea House, 1994. The story of "the Material Girl," her rise to stardom, and her life as one of the most successful female entertainers in history.

Anthony DeCurtis and James Henke with Holly George-Warren, eds., *The Rolling Stone Illustrated History of Rock.* New York: Random House, 1992. A definitive history of rock music with profiles by top rock critics of the most important artists and musical styles.

Ron Frankl, *Bruce Springsteen.* New York: Chelsea House, 1994. The life and times of "the Boss" and the story of his success.

Karen Marie Graves, *Michael Jackson.* San Diego: Lucent Books, 2001. The often-troubled life of one of the most successful—and controversial—modern entertainers.

Tricia Henry, *Break All the Rules: Punk Rock and the Making of a Style.* Ann Arbor, MI: UMI Research Press, 1989. The history of punk rock during the 1970s, with many quotes and song lyrics from the people who created the style.

Stuart A. Kallen, *The Importance of John Lennon.* San Diego: Lucent Books, 2002. The life and times of one of rock's most influential musicians, including his early life in Liverpool, the success of the Beatles, and his solo career.

———, *The Rolling Stones.* San Diego: Lucent Books, 1999. A biography of the group and individuals who make up one of the world's most successful rock bands.

Sean Piccoli, *Jimi Hendrix.* New York: Chelsea House, 1997. The brief and shining career of one of the most gifted guitarists who ever graced a stage.

Adam Woog, *Elvis Presley.* San Diego: Lucent Books, 1997. A biography of the king from his dirt-poor childhood to his glory days as one of the world's most successful entertainers.

———, *The History of Rock and Roll.* San Diego: Lucent Books, 1999. The evolution of rock music from its roots in the fifties to the present.

• Works Consulted •

Books

Fred Bronson, *The Billboard Book of Number One Hits*. New York: Billboard Publications, 1988. *Billboard* is a trade magazine dedicated to the music and entertainment business. It introduced the first music popularity chart in 1940, and by the 1950s the magazine featured a weekly list of the one hundred top-selling songs. With twenty listings, the Beatles have the most number-one hits in the book.

Jim DeRogatis, *Kaleidoscope Eyes*. New York: Citadel, 1996. A well-informed exploration of psychedelic rock from the 1960s to the 1990s written by a senior editor of *Rolling Stone*.

Gillian G. Gaar, *She's a Rebel*. Seattle: Seal, 1992. The history of women in rock and roll from the 1950s to the 1990s.

Mikal Gilmore, *Night Beat*. New York: Anchor Books, 1998. A collection of rock criticism, interviews, and record reviews that span the twenty-year career of one of rock's most respected authors, who has written extensively for the rock journal *Rolling Stone*.

Michael Gray, *Song and Dance Man III*. London: Cassell, 2000. A weighty and intellectual assessment of Bob Dylan's songs with an analysis of his lyrics and much speculation about the singer's various motives and inspirations.

Gerri Hirshey, *Nowhere to Run*. New York: Times Books, 1984. The story of sixties soul music as told through the lives of Ray Charles, Aretha Franklin, the Temptations, and dozens of other black artists.

George Martin, *With a Little Help from My Friends: The Making of Sgt. Pepper*. New York: Little, Brown, 1994. This book details the technical and creative processes behind the Beatles' most highly acclaimed masterpiece, written by the producer who was instrumental in shaping those sounds.

Linda Martin and Kerry Segrave, *Anti-Rock*. Hamden, CT: Archon Books, 1988. A history of the resistance to, and censorship of, rock music by politicians, clergy, parents, and law-enforcement authorities.

Jack McDonough, *San Francisco Rock*, San Francisco: Chronicle Books, 1985. A detailed exploration of rock music in the City by the Bay between 1965 and 1985 with biographies of dozens of fascinating personalities, hundreds of great photographs, and color reprints of psychedelic posters.

William McKeen, ed., *Rock and Roll Is Here to Stay*. New York: W.W. Norton, 2000. An anthology of rock history and commentary by renowned writers and rock luminaries such as Patti Smith, Salman Rushdie, Tom Wolfe, Frank Zappa, and many others.

James Miller, *Flowers in the Dustbin: The Rise of Rock and Roll, 1947–1977*. New York: Simon and Schuster, 1999. A well-researched exploration of the first thirty years of rock by a respected rock critic.

Philip Norman, *Shout*. New York: Simon and Schuster, 1981. The definitive biography on the Beatles, from their childhood lives in Liverpool through their years as chart-topping rock royalty, written by a journalist from the *London Times* who traveled with the group extensively during the late 1960s.

Robert K. Oermann, *A Century of Country*. New York: TV Books, 1999. The richly illustrated story of the people who made country music what it is today, based on the Nashville Network's thirteen-part documentary series.

Tricia Rose, *Black Noise*. Hanover, NH: Wesleyan University Press, 1994. An in-depth exploration of rap music and hip-hop culture.

Gene Sculatti and Davin Seay, *San Francisco Nights*. New York: St. Martin's, 1985. This book focuses on the psychedelic music revolution in the Bay Area that exploded during three short years from 1965 to 1968; it also contains information about the Grateful Dead, Janis Joplin, Jefferson Airplane, and others.

Pete Shotten and Nicholas Schaffner, *John Lennon in My Life*. New York: Stein and Day, 1983. An insider's perspective of the former Beatle by a man who first met John Lennon at the age of five. Shotten and Lennon remained extremely close friends until the musician's death in 1980.

David P. Szatmary, *Rockin' in Time: A Social History of Rock and Roll*. New York: Schirmer Books, 2000. The social history of rock and roll that focuses on the African American contributions to the style, from its ancient tribal roots to hip hop.

Don Waller, *The Motown Story*. New York: Charles Scribner's Sons, 1985. The history of the record company that produced the Supremes, the Temptations, Michael Jackson, and others.

Ed Ward, Geoffrey Stokes, and Ken Tucker, *Rock of Ages: The Rolling Stone History of Rock*. New York: Rolling Stone, 1986. An in-depth exploration of rock music, culture, and business written by renowned rock journalists and published by *Rolling Stone* magazine.

Jann Wenner, ed., *20 Years of Rolling Stone: What a Long, Strange Trip It's Been*. New York: Straight Arrow, 1987. A history of rock music, culture, and stars from the viewpoint of *Rolling Stone* magazine.

Periodicals

David Bauder, "New Game Is Blowin' on the Web," *Los Angeles Times,* February 22, 2002.

Robert Hillburn, "They Said She Couldn't Do It," *Los Angeles Times,* June 21, 1998.

Mark Jacobson, "Chuck Berry, the Father of Rock Turns Seventy-Five," *Rolling Stone,* December 6, 2001.

Internet Sources

The Andy Warhol Homepage, "The Andy Warhol Biography." www.warhol.dk.

Stephen Thomas Erlewine, "The Sex Pistols," AMG All Music Guide. www.allmusic.com.

———, "Soundgarden," AMG All Music Guide. www.allmusic.com.

———, "U2," AMG All Music Guide, www.allmusic.com.

———, "Thriller," AMG All Music Guide. www.allmusic.com.

Hoy Hoy, "Wynonie Harris," www.hoyhoy.com.

James Brown Enterprises, "James Brown: The Godfather of Soul," 2001. www.godfatherofsoul.com,

Rollingstone.com, "Public Enemy Biography," 2002. www.rollingstone.com.

———, "Talking Heads Biography," 2002. www.rollingstone.com.

Salon. www.salon.com.

Fraser White, "Blondie Archive: Biography," April 26, 2000. http://blondie.ausbone.net.

The Woody Guthrie Foundation and Archives, "Woody Guthrie," 2001. www.woodyguthrie.org.

• Index •

• Picture Credits •

Cover: Denis O'Regan/CORBIS
© AFP/CORBIS, 9
© Jeff Albertson/CORBIS, 88
©Bettmann/CORBIS, 56, 70
© CORBIS,94
© Getty Images,15, 18, 20, 21, 24, 30

(both), 31, 35,38, 44, 47, 57, 59, 66, 67, 79, 80, 92, 94, 99
© Hulton-Deutsch Collection/COR-BIS, 13, 28
Stuart A. Kallen, 63, 78, 81
© Neal Preston/CORBIS,75, 78

• About the Author •

Stuart A. Kallen is the author of more than 150 nonfiction books for children and young adults. He has written on topics ranging from the theory of relativity to rock-and-roll history to life on the American frontier. In addition, Mr. Kallen has written award-winning children's videos and television scripts. In his spare time, Stuart A. Kallen is a singer-songwriter-guitarist in San Diego, California.